STREET NAI
MILTON KEYNES
WEST

STREET NAMES OF MILTON KEYNES WEST

ANNE BAKER

Phillimore

2006

Published by
PHILLIMORE & CO. LTD
Shopwyke Manor Barn, Chichester, West Sussex, England
phillimore.co.uk

ISBN 1-86077-410-5
ISBN 13 978-1-86077-410-2

Printed and bound in Great Britain by
THE CROMWELL PRESS
Trowbridge, Wiltshire

CONTENTS

ACKNOWLEDGEMENTS

I would like to thank John Platt, former Secretary to the Board of Milton Keynes Development Corporation, for agreeing to write the Foreword to this book and, as the man originally charged with the task of naming the streets of the new city, making the project possible in the first place. Also Liz Preston, Milton Keynes City Discovery Centre; Zena Flinn, the Living Archive, Wolverton and Ruth Meardon, the Local Studies Centre, Milton Keynes Library. All those who provided photographs, including David Watts and staff of the Centre for Buckinghamshire Studies; Brett Thorn, Buckinghamshire Museum; Emma Butterfield, the National Portrait Gallery and Scott Grace. Also, thank you to my family for their support and encouragement and, last but not least, to my husband John, who wrote the Introduction to this book and helped in so many ways before he died in November 2004.

Dedication

In memory of my husband
John Anthony Baker
1935-2004

FOREWORD

There is a wealth of history in the names in Milton Keynes. They act as a daily reminder of the people who lived in the area through the ages, their way of life, their use of the land and the skills and trades they practised. Sir Frank Markham, in his introduction to the first volume of his *History of Milton Keynes and District* (1973), hoped that the new generation in Milton Keynes might 'wish to know of its past, and to retain the best of it'. Sir Frank was a great believer in the continuity of communities and the value of roots. He had been an opponent of the proposal to build a new town in North Buckinghamshire, but, faced with the decision to go ahead, he and a number of other local people sought to engage with the planners in order to have new development complement the existing settlements. They were particularly anxious to see Stony Stratford and the villages incorporated into the new city in a form they would find acceptable and to make the new city something of which they, too, could be proud. Happily for all concerned, as Michael Reed, later one of the founding Directors of the City Discovery Centre, noted in *The Buckinghamshire Landscape* (1979), the Development Corporation took 'an enlightened attitude towards conservation'.

I remember back in 1973 Sir Frank and Lady Markham walking with Fred Roche, Stuart Mosscrop and Chris Woodward, round the area of the Secklow Mound and down the quiet green lane that ran from Bradwell Common to the Great Linford-Little Woolstone road. Sir Frank, who wanted to impress on the Corporation the long history of the area and the role of the Secklow Hundred as a 'centre of government', was greatly encouraged by the willingness of the designers to listen to his enthusiastic presentation of the past. One of those on this walk was a devotee of the theory of ley lines and would later propose the 'midsummer solstice' pattern of naming for the boulevards. Sir Frank wrote to me in October 1974, a year before he died, expressing the hope 'that my work may in some way help to produce a fine civic consciousness in the great new city'. He never saw the city centre, but I am sure he would have been delighted with the naming of the boulevards and with the incorporation of the Secklow Mound behind the Library.

The names found in Milton Keynes are by no means all from the growth of the new city. Areas like Bradwell, Fenny Stratford, Loughton and Stony Stratford, to name but a few, all contain road names from long before the designation of a new city. So, it was only sensible that, from the beginning, the Development Corporation should have taken naming seriously and welcomed, in 1968, an approach from Newport Pagnell RDC on the question of preserving the history of the area when identifying elements of the new city. Bob Dunbabin, the Clerk of Newport Pagnell RDC, and Ray Bellchambers, then a member of the RDC and a Corporation Board Member, were particularly keen to see the old merged into the new. The Corporation indicated its willingness to take the initiative on naming and I (with a more than passing interest in history) was deputed to do the work. The Local Authorities Joint Liaison Committee endorsed the proposal that the Corporation should take the lead and one of our first acts was to send Sue Godber to see Mr Shirley at Peartree Farm, Woughton-on-the-Green, to collect field names; Eaglestone was one of the fruits of this visit.

A small group of MKDC Board Members (Ray Bellchambers, Margaret Durbridge and Jim Cassidy), with a highways engineer (John Rowlands) and myself, devised and put forward the proposals for naming the city areas and the city's H and V roads, and the Board of the Development Corporation cleared the proposals before they were submitted to the local authorities, which had the legal responsibility for such matters. Nearly all the proposals made by the Corporation were accepted, although Wolverton UDC was not happy with the name Hodge Furze and requested a change to Hodge Lea. Those of us who liked the idea of naming the city centre Secklow were over-ruled before any proposals left the Corporation. The local authorities, particularly Newport Pagnell RDC and UDC and Wolverton UDC, played a very helpful part in the process, being keen to conserve all sensible links between the past and the new city's future. Bletchley UDC, which, in my view, was never very enthusiastic about the Development Corporation's role, was unwilling to see defined and named areas created within the UDC boundaries or to anticipate the naming and navigational needs of the wider city road system.

Naming the 'city roads' and CMK 'gates' was one opportunity to conserve long gone aspects of local history, such as Secklow (914), Snelshall Priory (12th century), the Portway (a 13th-century route to Newport), and Groveway (1781). I remember taking the name for Dansteed Way from Dansteed Furlong (Dunstead 1641), mentioned in the book *The Roman Roads of South-East England*. The archaeologists had not yet discovered an ancient settlement in the area – but there was indeed a 'place on the hill', as Dennis Mynard was later happy to tell me! If Dr Margaret Gelling had published her book *Place-Names in the Landscape* (1984) twenty years earlier, we would have been better equipped to spot more significant names from the past.

To 'name' an urban area the size of Milton Keynes was not an easy task. As the opening of new areas and the building of houses gathered pace, the co-operation of developers had to be sought. Some of them were wont to use unimaginative 'catalogue lists' of names for their schemes, which they repeated in towns all over the country. We were ably supported by the new Milton Keynes Borough Council in our efforts to broaden the developers' horizons, the Council sharing our desire to see varied and interesting names adopted. We sought to introduce 'different' themes, particularly in the early years. The Corporation broke new ground with the landscaping of Milton Keynes; we tried in our small way to bring some variety into the naming too.

Pleasing everybody is, of course, impossible, names being a matter of personal taste. It has to be borne in mind that even names low down in the order of things – such as a small residential close on the edge of Milton Keynes – have to be unique if confusion is to be avoided in postal and traffic terms. Producing around 2,000 of them between 1970 and 1992 was not easy; they all had to be cleared by the appropriate councillor as well as by the Council itself. Where did the new city's names come from? Well, many backgrounds, as Anne Baker has recorded so carefully. In the villages history was the usual basis and the Heritage Map (1983), compiled by Bob Croft and Brian Giggins, shows the background to some of the historical names used in the city. Elsewhere themes were selected from which suitable names could emerge, as at Heelands where it was decided to use names from the North-West Yorkshire Highlands, an area with which one of those responsible had a personal family link. Myrtle Bank (Stacey Bushes) reminded me of a hotel in Kingston, Jamaica. Other names were reminiscent of far-flung places known to those involved (in one case a distant holiday home). The 'rock stars' theme at Crownhill was suggested by a local resident who was a member of the Elvis Presley Fan Club, Elvis being 'the King'. Ray Bellchambers made a number of suggestions for names in the Stantonbury and Bradwell areas. The names in Campbell Park were selected in appreciation of the role of Lord Campbell of Eskan in the development of Milton Keynes. Many people made contributions to the bank of names.

Sometimes there were objections. One university-educated resident complained to Wolverton UDC that the name 'Blackdown' at Fullers Slade had unfortunate racial connotations and was unacceptable; he was apparently unaware that the theme was hills and that the Blackdown Hills are in Devon. On another occasion I was asked why such a boringly ordinary name as 'William Smith Close' was used at Woolstone; explanation of the importance of William Smith and his steam plough put that right. Milton Keynes Parish Council invited me to a meeting to explain why such unknown and irrelevant names had been put forward for their village; again, explanation of the historical context of the names was accepted by the villagers. A sign of the times was a reluctance in the early 1970s to see one name attached to a road with both rental and sale housing schemes on it – or even to see the schemes sharing the same access road! By the 1980s such views had disappeared. At Kiln Farm, where the names were in place before many occupants arrived, I received a strong reaction to the spine road being called 'Pitfield'; in this case, the names had been officially approved, but I was told in very straight terms how detrimental to marketing a name like 'Pitfield' would be. I still cannot see the problem (it was after all an old brickmaking area, hence Brickkiln Farm). No London banks seemed to find an address in 'Cheapside' a disadvantage.

One of the last naming tasks I undertook personally, together with highways engineer John Wardley, was the naming of the city road roundabouts. If anyone I meet – in places far from Milton Keynes – has been to the new city, it is the roundabouts they talk about. Despite the Corporation's Information Unit producing city road maps from 1975 and placing Information Boards (incorporating maps) in lay-bys at the entrances to the Designated Area from 1976, the H and V roads and the roundabouts have always defeated some sections of society. We discovered early in the development that lorry drivers mastered map-reading and the navigation system fairly quickly, but those with high-powered cars or higher education found them difficult!

It is hard to believe that it is nearly forty years since the new city project began and it is heartening to see a book incorporating the results of what was essentially a 'backroom' task among the complex and highly technical responsibilities of the Development Corporation. It would be remiss of me not to take the opportunity to acknowledge the contributions made by Ralph Bailey (BMK) and Teresa Jenkins and Val Sharpe (MKDC) over a long period. In addition to their real jobs, they coped with the naming of roads in a multitude of housing developments throughout the new city – a sometimes thankless task, although fascinating to look back on. I also remember well the kindness and support received in the early days from the late Colin Rees, when he was Wolverton UDC's Chief Engineer, and the co-operation received over many years from Dennis Mynard and the staff of the Archaeology Unit.

JOHN PLATT

Secretary to the Board of the
Milton Keynes Development Corporation 1983-92

INTRODUCTION
by John Baker

When in 1967 nearly forty square miles of North Buckinghamshire countryside was designated for the building of Britain's biggest New Town, it was a decision which stirred the emotions of people then living in the three towns and 13 villages in the area.

Many people, particularly those in the northern towns of Wolverton and Stony Stratford, were totally opposed to the concept. Ten miles south, however, the majority of Bletchley residents were far more welcoming, living as they did under an urban authority which had been involved in building 'overspill' accommodation, mainly for Londoners, since shortly after the end of the Second World War.

In 1962, Buckinghamshire's chief architect and planning officer, Fred Pooley, had produced proposals for a city in which the transport system would be based on a monorail with townships of up to 7,000 people built along the route and with no homes more than seven minutes' walk from a station. The object of Pooley's vision was instantly tagged 'Pooleyville' by the local press.

It has been said that Pooley's vision 'laid the foundations' for a future city, although initially it produced considerable squabbling among national, county and local politicians during the early years of the 1960s. This makes it all the more surprising to recall that, by early 1966, the concept finally came into focus in the shape of a map produced by Richard Crossman, Labour's Minister of Housing and Local Government at that time. It revealed an area (later reduced after a public inquiry to 21,900 acres, roughly 34 square miles) on which it was planned to build the biggest New Town of them all, with a population of a quarter of a million people.

Suddenly, speed was of the essence.

Within a matter of months, the Draft North Buckinghamshire New Town (Designation Order) was made and announced by Anthony Greenwood, who had succeeded Crossman. The name Milton Keynes was chosen from one of the villages in the area – a choice strongly supported by Lord Campbell of Eskan, the first appointed Chairman of Milton Keynes Development Corporation, as acknowledging the hybrid of the poet Milton and the internationally acclaimed economist, John Maynard Keynes.

With the appointment of the Main Consultants, Llewelyn-Davies Weeks Forestier-Walker and Bor, and members of the Board of the Corporation, concentration was focused on establishing the key issues affecting the widest range of planning and social objectives, the goals of architects and engineers, the search for vital decisions over the vexed question of the city's transport system, projected housing densities and the siting and size of the new main shopping centre.

Problems on a scale never before encountered were overcome, one by one, as a direct result of the involvement of many of the country's finest planners, architects and engineers gathered together by a Corporation determined to meet the challenges and opportunities presented to make the venture the success it has undoubtedly become.

The Plan for Milton Keynes, which followed an Interim Report a year earlier, was produced for limited distribution among Board members and senior officers late in 1969. Its two volumes were formally launched at a press conference the following March and a Public Inquiry, lasting ten days, took place towards the end of June.

Opposition to the Plan had by now largely dissipated as work began on putting in the first phases of the city's infrastructure. The grid road system as we know it today, started with a section of the H2 (Millers Way) east of the V7 (Saxon Street), there were presentations of plans for specific areas, the first MKDC housing schemes got underway at Simpson and in Stony Stratford, the Open University arrived at Walton Hall, and proposals for the central area of Bletchley and for the two northern towns were presented.

It was all systems go. Then came the shock announcement that the little village of Cublington, near Wing, had been listed among the possible sites for the third London airport. The impact of this news sent shockwaves through most people living in North Buckinghamshire. A poll conducted by the *Milton Keynes Gazette* revealed that more than 90 per cent opposed the plan, which would also have the effect of turning Milton Keynes into an airport city.

The Hon. Mr Justice Roskill, chairing the Commission of Inquiry into the siting of the airport, published plans which would lead to the expansion of Milton Keynes westwards from Bletchley, through Winslow, to provide for a population of more than 400,000 people.

Lord Campbell, who was to earn the soubriquet of 'the father of Milton Keynes', led the fight, strongly supported by press and public, against the proposal which became, for him, a resignation issue. In evidence to the Commission, he went as far as to suggest that grafting an airport onto that part of Milton Keynes which would have been developed by 1987, 'could only produce a mongrel city'. He was subsequently joined in opposition by Professor Colin Buchanan, an architect and town planner who was also a Commission member. His dissenting report ultimately saved the city as we know it today.

Cublington was dropped by the government from the list of possible sites in April 1971 and over the past two decades the plan has become reality.

Development on this scale could only have come about as a result of the participants' belief in the Plan and their collective and individual belief in their abilities, led by a man who was a passionate believer in Milton Keynes.

THE GRID ROADS

The main thoroughfares through Milton Keynes are designed in the pattern of a grid, each square enclosing an estate. The grid roads are numbered vertically – V 1-11 called Streets, and horizontally – H 1-10 called Ways. Even before Roman times, there were several ancient trackways crossing the area which is now Milton Keynes, particularly from west to east, and most of the H Ways have taken their names.

Snelshall Street (V 1)   Refers to Snelshall Priory which stood about a mile and a half to the south-west of nearby Whaddon church. The priory was founded in about 1219 and stood in 11 acres of surrounding countryside.

Tattenhoe Street (V 2)   Named after the tiny village of Tattenhoe, now incorporated in the Tattenhoe area of Milton Keynes. The site of the Norman homestead of Tattenhoe has been preserved.

Fulmer Street (V 3)   Meaning 'the foul mere', Fulmer takes its name from an ancient pond at Shenley Brook End. Also, Fulmoor Close is marked on a 1771 Plan and Survey of Shenley as a field owned by William Brice.

Watling Street (V 4)   This is the section of the old Roman road between Fenny Stratford and Stony Stratford. Until the arrival of Milton Keynes, it was a stretch of the A5 until a new section of the A5 was constructed in the 1970s so that through traffic could have an uninterrupted passage through the new city. The name Watling Street derives from the ninth-century *Waeclinga straet,* meaning 'a Roman road identified with the followers of a man called Wacol', believed to have been centred around St Albans, an early name for which was *Waeclingaceaster.*

Great Monks Street (V 5)   Passes by Bradwell Abbey following the route of an old track along which the monks once traversed.

Grafton Street (V 6)   In the 18th century the Dukes of Grafton (family name Fitzroy) held substantial lands and property in south Northamptonshire, owning several local villages including Deanshanger and Paulerspury. They had a great mansion, Wakefield Lodge, near Potterspury, about a mile from Stony Stratford, where, according to Frank Markham in his *History of Milton Keynes and District*, the Graftons did most of their shopping and tipped the tradesmen with braces of pheasant or partridge. Descended from Charles II, the 3rd Duke was Prime Minister 1768-9 and the 4th Duke (1821-1918) was a well-known local figure.

Saxon Street (V 7)   This street leads to and passes through the centre of Milton Keynes, which is built at the highest point in the area and on the site of Secklow Corner, the ancient Saxon meeting place of the Secklow Hundred.

Marlborough Street (V 8)   The Dukes of Marlborough were associated with the Milton Keynes area after Sarah, Duchess of Marlborough purchased the Stantonbury estates in 1727. She gave it to her grandson, John Spencer, and the lands remained in the ownership of the Earls Spencer of Althorp, Northamptonshire until well into the 19th century. Marlborough Street begins at Stantonbury and skirts the east side of the modern estate.

Overstreet (V 9)   Following the line of a 17th-century track near Downs Barn, this is a short stretch of carriageway connecting Campbell Park with Great Linford. The affix *Over* usually indicates a place 'at the ridge or slope'.

Brickhill Street (V 10)   Named after the villages of Little, Great and Bow Brickhill from where this street begins on its journey northwards to meet the Wolverton road at Great Linford. It replaces an ancient road which ran beside the river Ouzel to Danesborough, an historic hill fort in the woods above Bow Brickhill. According to the *Oxford Dictionary of English Place Names,* Brickhill has nothing to do with bricks, but derives from the Celtic *brig* meaning 'hill top' and the Old English *hyll.*

Tongwell Street (V 11)   Named after the field on which stood Tongwell Farm, shown on an 1806 map of Newport Pagnell. Tongwell Street runs from Old Farm Park to the outskirts of Newport Pagnell.

Ridgeway (H 1)   This is a short section of the prehistoric Ridgeway track which ran from Avebury on Salisbury Plain to the east coast at the Wash.

Millers Way (H 2)   This was the first of the new city roads to be built. It follows the line of an old track which ran between Bradwell windmill and Stony Stratford, hence the name Millers Way.

Monks Way (H 3)   Skirting the site of Bradwell Abbey, this name refers to the monks which once inhabited the abbey and traversed the tracks and pathways in the area.

Dansteed Way (H 4)   Danstead was an ancient site and field name, 'Long Danstead and Short Danstead', shown on a 1678 plan of the area. It is tempting to suggest that the site may have been a homestead occupied by the Danes, but excavations carried out in 1979-81 revealed it to be the site of an Iron-Age/Saxon village. There were, however, many savage raids by the Danes in the early 1000s AD, including an invasion of Newport Pagnell, and several Danish settlements in the area now covered by Milton Keynes. The road runs from Grange Farm in the west to Newport Pagnell.

Portway (H 5)   A Roman route running from Whaddon, through Shenley and Seckloe, to Willen was known by AD 1250 as 'Rector's Portway', and 'Dichefurlong by Portwei'. The new thoroughfare which has taken its name follows close to the old track. Port, meaning a town, or market town, identifies this as 'the way to town' i.e. Newport Pagnell.

Childs Way (H 6)   This takes its name from an 18th-century track and field name in east Loughton, by which the road passes on its way from Shenley Common Farm in the east to the M1 at junction 14. An archaic meaning of child (or childe) was a young nobleman. Alternatively, someone named Child(s) may have owned or farmed land in Loughton.

Chaffron Way (H 7)   This was the name of an 18th-century track through Woughton, by which the modern Chaffron Way passes. A chaffron, or chamfron, is a piece of leather or plate of steel worn by a horse to protect its face in battle. The reason for its use here is obscure.

Standing Way (H 8)   This follows the route of an ancient track which, it is believed, linked Buckingham, via Thornborough, to Watling Street and the Roman station of Magiovinium near Fenny Stratford. Today it is the A421, which runs from Buckingham to the A1, east of Bedford. The name Standing may be a derivation of the Old English word *staning* meaning 'stony places'.

Groveway (H 9)   Groveway has been in existence and called by this name since at least the 18th century. It travels from Watling Street at Bletchley to the north side of Wavendon, where it gives way to the ancient London road, coming in from Hockliffe, through Woburn and on to Newport Pagnell. Presumably it once passed through the groves of walnut and other trees which grew in this area.

Bletcham Way (H 10)   This was the name of another 18th-century track which passed through Woughton. The name derives from *Blecca's-ham*, the Old English meaning 'homestead of a man called Blecca'. The present road runs from Bletchley to Wavendon Gate.

A Note on OS Map References

The Ordnance Survey (OS) numbers referred to are taken from the Milton Keynes Development Corporation's paper *Names in Milton Keynes* (1992) and are from a 1:2500 scale edition updated in 1965. A collection of old maps may be seen, by appointment, at Milton Keynes City Discovery Centre, Bradwell Abbey, or at the Local Studies Centre, Central Milton Keynes Library.

WEST

LOUGHTON

KNOWLHILL

SHENLEY CHURCH END

SHENLEY LODGE

WOODHILL

SHENLEY BROOK END

FURZTON

WESTCROFT

EMERSON VALLEY

TATTENHOE

EMERSON VALLEY

On a poll of Buckinghamshire freeholders taken in 1784, Thomas Emerson is listed as owning land in Shenley and Bletchley. Emerson Valley combines the names of two farms in the Shenley area. Emerson Farm is late 17th- or early 18th-century and Valley Farm, on Tattenhoe Road from Shenley Brook End, dates from the 17th century.

Emerson Farm (left) and Valley Farm (right) at Shenley Brook End. Combined, the two names gave rise to Emerson Valley.

THEME Valleys and places associated with them

Alstone Field   Alstonfield is a pretty village in the Dove Valley of the Peak District. It has a shop, a pub and several interesting buildings, including the church which has old carved oak box pews, one of which was poet Charles Cotton's family pew.

Appleton Mews   Appleton-le-Moors and Appleton-le-Street in North Yorkshire are neighbouring villages on the edge of the Vale of Pickering.

Archford   Archford Moor and barrow (ancient burial mound) is above the Dove Valley on the borders of Staffordshire and Derbyshire.

Austwick Lane   Austwick is a village on the A65, south of Newby in the Wenning Valley.

Banktop Place   In Darlington, Durham there is a Bank Top station which is known as 'the birthplace of the railway' and is where Stephenson's first steam engine stands. Darlington is in the valley of the river Tees. A 19th-century map of North Yorkshire shows a hamlet called Bank Top in the old coalmining region near Halifax.

Barkestone Close   Barkestone-le-Vale is a village in the Vale of Belvoir, a few miles north-west of Belvoir Castle.

Belvoir Avenue   For some reason pronounced 'Beaver', when in fact the name derives from the French *bel* (beautiful) and *voir* (to see), the Vale of

Belvoir in Leicestershire is wolden countryside dominated by Belvoir Castle standing on a high spur above dense woodland. The castle was originally built in the 11th century, fell to ruin in the 16th century and was recreated in medieval castle style by the Dukes of Rutland in the early 19th century. It is still the home of the Duke and Duchess of Rutland.

Beresford Close   Beresford Hall at Beresford Dale in the Dove Valley of Derbyshire was the home of the 17th-century poet, Charles Cotton. There is a fishing lodge, built by Cotton in 1674, which is now known as the Fishing Temple. Beresford Vale is considered to be one of the prettiest areas along the Dove river.

Bingham Rise   Bingham is a small town in Nottinghamshire on the edge of the Vale of Belvoir.

Birchenlee   Birchinlee in the Derwent Valley was a village built in 1901 to house the navvies building the Derwent Reservoir and constructing the Howden and Derwent dams. The village stood halfway up the road on the west side of Howden Reservoir. It housed about 900 families and had a shop, village hall, school, chapel and a hospital.

Bottesford Close   Bottesford is a large, scattered village in the Vale of Belvoir, closely linked with the castle. Many former Masters of the Belvoir Hunt are buried in the village churchyard of St Mary the Virgin. There are also monuments to the 7th and 8th Earls of Rutland by Grinling Gibbons, as well as a monument to two Rutland infants who died from a 'loathsome disease' blamed on local witches who were tried and hanged. The village, on the banks of the river Devon, still has a stocks and whipping post.

Bowland Drive   The Forest of Bowland, Lancashire is a designated Area of Outstanding Natural Beauty. Covering 310 square miles, with the rivers Lune, Ribble, Wyre and Hodder running through, its wild fells are steeped in mystery and legend. The Trough of Bowland is a wild, heather-banked pass and the only road to cross the lonely forest.

Bradley Grove   Which of several villages in Britain named Bradley was intended here is not known. The most likely candidates seem to be Bradley, a village in Coverdale in the Yorkshire Dales, or Bradley Stoke, which is to the north of Bristol in the Severn Valley. Once a hamlet where cattle grazed, this has in recent years been developed into the largest private housing estate in Europe.

Burholme   Burholme is an area in the Lower Hodder Valley near the Trough of Bowland, where Burholme Bridge crosses the river Dunsop, and Burholme Farm is now the property of the Duchy of Lancaster.

Cardwell Close   Cardwell, near Gourock, Renfrewshire, Scotland lies on the Firth of Clyde.

Chieveley Court   Chieveley is just off the M4 north of Newbury, in the vale of the Berkshire Downs.

Chingle Croft   Chingle Hall is an historic house north of Preston, near the village of Goosnargh, at the southern edge of Longridge Fell, Lancashire. It was built around 1210 for Adam de Singleton and is said to be the most haunted house in Britain. Its 16 ghosts include that of Eleanor Singleton, last in the family line. The house also has several priest holes.

Chipping Vale   An actual 'Chipping Vale' does not seem to exist. It could refer to the Cotswolds area around Chipping Norton and Chipping Campden, or to the upland moors and fells around the village of Chipping in the Hodder Valley of Lancashire. The name Chipping is derived from the Old English *ceping,* meaning 'a market-place'.

Coldeaton Lane   Cold Eaton is a village in the Derbyshire Dales, lying about two miles north-west of Alsop-le-Dale.

Colston Bassett   Famed for its association with fine cheese, Colston Bassett is a village at the western end of the Vale of Belvoir on the river Smite. A stone bridge over the river leads to Colston Hall, built in 1704, and the ruins of St Mary's church, which was replaced in 1892 by a lavish new edifice at the behest of the lord of the manor, Robert Millington Knowles.

Cropton Rise   Cropton is a village in the Vale of Pickering. In 1984 a small brewery was started in the cellars of the *New Inn* and by 1996 Cropton Brewery was established in purpose-built accommodation on a farm behind the pub.

Cropwell Bishop   Cropwell Bishop is another Vale of Belvoir village, a few miles from Colston Bassett.

Crosslow Bank   Cross Low is an area on the edge of the parish of 'the Plague village' of Eyam in Derbyshire, in the Derwent Valley.

Culmstock Close   Culmstock is a town lying north of Sidmouth by the river Culm in the Culm Valley in Devon, south of the Blackdown Hills.

Denchworth Court   Denchworth is an Oxfordshire village in the Vale of White Horse, north of Wantage, about halfway between Oxford and Swindon.

Eastbury Court   Eastbury is a village in Berkshire, on the edge of the Lambourn Downs.

Eddington Court   Edington, near Chippenham in Wiltshire, lies in the vale of the Marlborough Downs. It was the scene of a battle in AD 878 between the Saxon troops of King Alfred of Wessex and the Danes under Guthran. The struggle was won by Alfred, whose troops chased the Danes back to the King's castle at Chippenham. There they were imprisoned and starved until they conceded defeat. It is a village of farms and meadows and has a very large church, originally built in 1351 by William of Edington, Bishop of Winchester and Treasurer to Edward III.

Ellerburn Place   Ellerburn is a pretty hamlet near Thornton-le-Dale, North

Yorkshire. It lies in a valley through the Tabular Hills, where there is a wildlife reserve. Ellerburn Bank is a butterfly and wild flower meadow.

Elmridge Court This possibly refers to Elm Ridge, an area of Darlington in the Tees Valley, where there is an Elm Ridge Garden Centre and Elm Ridge Methodist Church, which was a 19th-century home of the Pease family until it was sold in 1932 and converted into the church.

Emmett Close This possibly refers to the Rev. William Edward Emmet, MA of Queen's College, Oxford, who held the living at Whaddon from 1902. The Rev. Percy Barnabas Emmet was a curate also living at the Vicarage.

Everley Close Everley is a village west of Scarborough, in the Vale of Pickering.

Fadmoor Place Fadmoor is a neighbouring village to Gillamoor on the edge of the North Yorkshire Moors.

Fernborough Haven Possibly this refers to the village of Farnborough in Berkshire, which lies in the vale of the Lambourn Downs.

Forches Close Forches Cross is a village near Barnstaple in the Whiddon Valley of north Devon.

Froxfield Court Froxfield in Wiltshire is three miles west of Hungerford on the Berkshire Downs, in the Kennet Valley. It is said that the Hounds of Hell can be seen on a moonlit night chasing the ghost of Wild Darnell across the fields of Froxfield. Darnell was the 16th-century owner of Littlecote House. (See Littlecote, Great Holm in *Street Names of Milton Keynes: North* for this story.)

Gillamoor Close Gillamoor is on the edge of the North Yorkshire Moors, at the southern end of Farndale, near Hutton-le-Hole.

Goathland Croft Goathland is a village in the middle of the North Yorkshire Moors. Five hundred feet above sea level, it is a major station on the Goathland and North Yorkshire Moors Railway. All the signs, lamps and features of the station are original, apart from the footbridge which was built about ten years ago. Goathland village features in the television series *Heartbeat*.

Gratton Court Gratton is a Derbyshire village in Gratton Dale near Cromford in the Derwent Valley. Gratton's Parlour is a natural cavern in the Black Rocks which rise above Cromford and Wirksworth and from which there are magnificent views over Matlock and Cromford.

Greenside Hill Greenside is a hamlet in the Forest of Bowland.

Greystoneley Lower Greystonely is a village in the Ribble Valley near Preston, Lancashire. It is the site of a wild boar park.

Grosmont Close Grosmont village is the next station after Goathland on the North Yorkshire Moors Railway, which was first opened in the 19th century and ran from Whitby to Pickering.

View across Emerson Valley towards Furzton.

Gundale Court   In the Vale of Pickering, Gundale Woods lie on the route of the North Yorkshire Railway as it passes through on its way to Levisham.

Hambleton Grove   The Hambleton Hills, North Yorkshire, run south from the west end of the Cleveland Hills, almost to the Vale of Pickering, with the Vale of York on their western side.

Harby Close   Harby village in the Vale of Belvoir stands close to the canal between Grantham and Nottingham and has the remains of an old wharf, windmill and granary barn.

Hareden Croft   The village of Hareden is on Sykes Fell, on the edge of the Forest of Bowland.

Hartington Grove   Hartington is another Dove Valley village. Hartington Hall, dating back to 1611, is a manor where, it is said, Bonnie Prince Charlie stayed in 1745 while on his march to London to seize the English crown.

Hawkshead Drive   Lying at the north end of Esthwaite Water, Hawkshead is a well-known Cumbrian village, famous for its knitwear. The poet William Wordsworth lived here as a boy and attended the local school. Several buildings in the village and the land around Esthwaite Water were given to the National Trust by Beatrix Potter, who lived two miles away at Near Sawrey.

Hazelhurst   Hazelhurst Fell is in the Forest of Bowland.

Hodder Lane   The Hodder river in West Yorkshire flows through the Hodder Valley.

Holton Hill   Of several possible places called Holton, the most likely seem to be Holton Lea, Dorset, which lies in the valleys of the rivers Piddle and Frome and is a Site of Special Scientific Interest where kingfishers and Sika deer may be seen; or Holton, Oxfordshire, a small, ancient village in the Thames Valley.

Hornby Chase   The river Wenning flows through Hornby, Lancashire, and from the stone bridge over the river there is a fine view of Hornby Castle high on a hill above. Built by the Normans, the castle was later aggrandised with the addition of towers and gargoyles by Sir Edward Stanley, who distinguished himself against the Scots at the Battle of Flodden in 1513 and was later dubbed Lord Monteagle by Henry VIII.

Keasdon Court   Keasdon is a village in the Wenning Valley, south-west of Austwick.

Lambourn Court   The Lambourn Downs and the Vale of Lambourn are in Berkshire, with the quaint little town of Lambourn in the middle. The downs are dotted with prehistoric burial mounds and traces of ancient field systems.

Lastingham Grove   Lastingham is a small village on the southern edge of the North Yorkshire Moors, close to North Riding Forest Park and the Vale of Pickering. In the main street there is a fountain which was built before 1100 and an inscription which records that St Cedd founded an abbey here in 654. The Danes destroyed the abbey in the ninth century but about 200 years later, at the request of the Abbot of Whitby, the crypt was rebuilt by William I and still survives in its original state.

Leigh Hill   Leigh Woods, Leigh Court and the village of Abbots Leigh are in the Avon Valley near Bristol. The village once belonged to the Abbey of St Augustine in Bristol. Leigh Court, originally built as a Tudor mansion in 1558, was demolished in 1812 and rebuilt in 1814 as a Palladian mansion by Philip Miles, a Bristol ship owner, banker and sugar baron. Today it is a privately owned conference and corporate entertainment centre.

Little Habton   Little Habton is a North Yorkshire village near Malton in the Vale of Pickering.

Lockton Court   Lockton is a small town on the A169 between Newton Dale and North Riding Forest, Yorkshire.

Manifold Lane   The Manifold river rises at Flash Head on Axe Edge above Buxton to wind its way southwards through the western side of the Peak District National Park and join the Dove river at Ilam. Less famous than its neighbouring Dove Valley, the Manifold Valley is no less beautiful.

Marshaw Place   Marshaw is a village in the Forest of Bowland, Lancashire. The river Wyre has its source on Marshaw Fell from where it flows down through the village on its 32½-mile journey to the sea at the Wyre estuary.

Newbridge Oval   There is a small town called Newbridge, midway between Woodstock in the Thames Valley and Wantage in the Vale of White Horse. Also, Newbridge in the Vale of Pickering is the gateway to the North Yorkshire Moors. The street is designed in an ovoid shape.

Newby Place   There are several villages called Newby in Cumbria and Yorkshire, but this probably refers to Newby village, Lancashire, on the A65 near Bentham in the Wenning Valley.

Nova Lodge   The only Nova Lodge located is a hotel in Thailand, which has no reason to be in Emerson Valley.

Oakenhead   This might refer either to Oakenhead Wood, in the Forest of Dean near Pillowell, in the Wye Valley area, or to Oakenhead Wood, Rawtenstall, in the Forest of Rossendale, Lancashire.

Peacock Hay   Peacock Hay is the name of an old, disused coal mine in the Staffordshire Potteries of the Trent Valley.

Pickering Drive   The Vale of Pickering is a broad trough of clay which separates the North Yorkshire Moors and the Yorkshire Wolds. The town of Pickering is at the southern foot of the moors.

Priors Park   In the Avon Valley and owned by the National Trust, Prior Park, Bath is an 18th-century landscaped garden, created by Ralph Allen with advice from the poet Alexander Pope and Lancelot (Capability) Brown.

Quantock Crescent   Where there are hills, there are valleys. The Quantock Hills in Somerset stretch from the coast at Watchet and Quantoxhead southwards to Taunton. The poets Wordsworth and Coleridge had a cottage at Nether Stowey among the wooded hills and gentle slopes, pastures and small villages of the Quantocks.

Ravenscar Court   Ravenscar is a village on the Yorkshire coast, lying between Whitby and Scarborough. 'Mad' King George III was treated here during his bouts of insanity at an asylum run by the Rev. Dr Francis Willis. The village's history goes back to Roman times and includes many smuggling tales.

Rillington Gardens   Rillington village lies on the A64 near Malton in the Vale of Pickering.

Roeburn Crescent   The Roeburn is a fast-flowing river, about 15 miles along the Lune Valley near Lancaster. It merges with the Wenning near Hornby.

Rusland Circus   Rusland is a village in Cumbria. It lies east of the southern end of lake Windermere in the Lake District.

Ryton Place   Ryton is a village in the Vale of Pickering on the river Rye.

Salton Link   Salton is a village in Ryedale, at the west end of the Vale of Pickering. In a wall, hidden by leafy overgrowth, is a sulphur well, the waters of which were once used for medicinal purposes and from which the local doctor filled bottles of water with which to treat his patients. This road is called Salton Link because it links Pickering Drive with Wenning Lane.

Sparsholt Close   There are two villages called Sparsholt: one is just outside Winchester in the Itchen Valley of Hampshire; the other, near Wantage in

Berkshire, is a pretty village with a very large medieval church on the edge of the Vale of White Horse.

Sutton Court   Sutton is a village in the Vale of Belvoir, north-west of Barkestone and just off the A52.

Sykes Croft   Sykes Fell is in the Forest of Bowland, with Sykes hamlet on the Trough of Bowland.

Taunton Deane   The Vale of Taunton Deane is on the west side of the Quantock Hills, Somerset, and lies between the Quantocks and Exmoor.

Thornley Croft   Thornley is a Durham village in the valley of the river Wear, north-west of Bishop Auckland.

Wardstone End   The Wardstone is a high peak in Lancashire, the highest summit on the Trough of Bowland, which stretches from Whitwell and across the moors to Abbeystead, taking in Gisburn Forest, the largest area of woodland in Lancashire. From the top of the Wardstone, the entire Lancashire coastline can be seen on a clear day.

Websters Meadow   Websters Meadow lies near Harden Fell in Lancashire, below Holme House Fell and Bleadale Fell.

Welburn Grove   Welburn is a small, pretty village in Ryedale, Vale of Pickering, and stands on the edge of the Castle Howard Estate. Little changed over the years, it has a church, a school, a village shop, a pub and a racing stables.

Wenning Lane   The Wenning Valley is part of Craven, which covers the southern area of the Yorkshire Dales National Park. The comparatively placid river Wenning flows through Bentham, the main town in the valley.

Wheatley Close   Wheatley, a small town east of Oxford, is on the river Thame and between the Vale of Aylesbury and the Vale of White Horse.

White Horse Drive   The Vale of White Horse lies between the Upper Thames Valley and the Berkshire Downs and runs from Oxford to Swindon. Its name derives from the White Horse of Uffington which was cut in the chalk hillside many hundreds of years ago. Nobody knows exactly when, but the preferred belief is that it is a late Bronze-Age representation of a Celtic horse goddess. Other theories suggest that it was cut in the fifth century AD by the Anglo-Saxon leader, Hengist, or that King Alfred ordered it in commemoration of his victory over the Danes in 871.

Winfold Lane   Winfold Fell lies in the Trough of Bowland, Lancashire.

Wolfscote Lane   Wolfscote Dale is near Alstonfield in the Dove Valley of Derbyshire.

Wray Court   Wray is a Lancashire village on the northern edge of the fells to the north-east of Lancaster. Old traders' routes cross the fells from Mill Houses near Wray to Slaidburn in Yorkshire.

Housing in Wardstone End, Emerson Valley.

Yalts Brow   As no Yalts Brow can be found, it is possible that Yatts Brow
was intended here. Yatts Brow Farm is in the hamlet of Yatts in the Vale of
Pickering.

FURZTON

*The name Furzton was taken from the old names of fields which previously
covered this area. 'Furze Ground' is shown on Ordnance Survey map 168
and, with 'Furze Field', on a 1771 plan and survey of part of the Lordship
of Shenley belonging to John Knapp Esq. 'Long Furze' is marked on
Ordnance Survey 21, and 'Brice's Furze' on Ordnance Survey 22 and
listed in a Shenley Estates sale catalogue dated 1903.*

THEME **Exmoor, where there are such names as Furzehill, Furze
Common and Fursdon, denoting an area covered by furze, or gorse**

Allerford Court   Allerford is a picturesque village in Porlock Vale, Somerset.
Homer Water flows through it and is crossed near the middle of the village
by a much photographed medieval packhorse bridge. The old school is used
as the local museum and paths through the green, wooded hillside lead up
to Selworthy Beacon.

Arlington Court   Arlington Court is a 3,500-acre estate in the valley of the
river Yeo near Barnstaple. The Victorian house, Arlington Court, is central
to the estate and has long been home of the Chichester family but is now
owned by the National Trust. It contains treasures collected by Miss Rosalie

Chichester on her many travels abroad, and in the working stable-yard there is a collection of 19th-century horse-drawn vehicles. There is also a large colony of Lesser Horseshoe bats.

Bampton Close   Bampton, on the mid-Devon/Somerset border, is at the centre of a village conservation area, with 100 listed buildings. With a long history steeped in the wool and pony trades, Bampton today is still central to sheep farming and is also famous for its floral displays. 'Bampton in Bloom' has won the National Britain in Bloom competition six times.

Barleycroft   In the south-east corner of Furzton, where a group of road names reflect the previous usage of the land, this was a small piece of arable land where barley was grown.

Barnstaple Court   Barnstaple is a town both ancient and modern, spoilt by the volume of traffic trying to pass through it. At the head of the estuary of the river Taw, it has less to do with Exmoor than with the sea, having been a commercial centre since 930 and a major port for trade with America in the 18th century. Among the town's historic sites are the Norman castle mound, the Long Bridge, first built in the 13th century, and the mid-19th-century Pannier Market.

Beacon Court   Beacon Point is a headland on the north Devon coast between Ilfracombe and Hele Bay. Further along the coastal path, between Heddons Mouth and Woody Bay, The Beacon is a Roman fortlet with the remains of a Roman signal station, preserved by the National Trust. Also, Beacon Castle is a settlement on a mound at the head of the Heddon Valley, above Parracombe.

Bickleigh Crescent   Bickleigh, on the river Exe just south of Tiverton, is a pretty village with thatched cottages and a 300-year-old bridge, said to have been the inspiration for the song *Bridge Over Troubled Water*. The old watermill is now a craft centre and Bickleigh Castle is a historic fortified manor on the edge of the village. Also nearby is Fursdon House, the ancestral home of the Fursdons, one of Devon's oldest families.

Bilbrook Lane   Bilbrook is a small village on the A39 on the northern fringe of the Brendon Hills in Somerset, one of a group of villages which include Washford and Carhampton, between the Brendon Hills and the Bristol Channel.

Blackmoor Gate   Blackmoor Gate is at the crossroads of the A39/A399 and is known as the Western Gateway to Exmoor. It lies on the old track of the Lynton to Barnstaple railway and the disused station is now a café.

Braybrooke Drive   In the south-east corner of Furzton, this name has a more local connection. Braybrooke Castle was in Northamptonshire; only the moat now remains. Closer to home, Robert de Braybrook acquired some land and the mill at Caldecotte from Geoffrey Chauncey in 1208. This then passed down to Gerard de Braybrook, who transferred it to John

Grey around 1293. Thereafter the mill and Caldecotte lands passed to his descendants, the de Greys de Wilton, lords of the manors of Water Eaton and Bletchley, which would have included the Furzton area. On Exmoor, the Bray river flows through Brayford and Bray Bridge before joining the rivers Mole and Taw.

Brendon Court   Brendon village is deep in the heart of *Lorna Doone* country and surprisingly far from the Brendon Hills. On the banks of the East Lynn river, this is one of Exmoor's 'exhibition' villages, with its old cottages and pub, its packhorse bridge over the babbling stream and the romance of the Doone Valley just a little way up stream.

Brushford Close   Brushford is a small village in the Barle Valley south of Dulverton. The name means 'ford by the bridge', from the Old English *brycg* and *ford*.

Buzzacott Lane   The Buzzacott Estate was part of the manor of Combe Martin, Devon, and Buzzacott Manor House is set back from the long approach road down from the moor to the village. The rocks around this part of Exmoor are rich in minerals and silver mines have been worked, intermittently, since the reign of Edward I. They were re-opened in 1837 and an adit and shaft of Buzzacott Mine remains as a site of interest to industrial archaeologists.

Calverleigh Crescent   Calverleigh is a small village just off the A361 north Devon holiday route near Tiverton. Set in lush farming country on the edge of Exmoor, Calverleigh House was built in 1844-5 for Joseph Chichester Nagle. The attractive church has a tower and font dating back to the 14th century and some late medieval stained glass is retained in the east window.

Carhampton Court   Carhampton, Somerset is on the A39 near Dunster. It is an ancient place of past importance, its name having been given to Carhampton Hundred. Its Saxon name was Carumtune, meaning 'farm at the place of the rocks'. Petty Sessions were being held there at least until 1868, and the church of St John the Baptist was restored by the Victorians. Today Carhampton is a thriving modern village with shops, sports and social clubs.

Challacombe   Challacombe is a scattered parish on the western fringe of Exmoor below Challacombe Common. It has a history of farming going back to the Bronze Age, with ancient field workings to prove it. From the 15th century the village and surrounding moorland was owned by the Fortescue Lordship. There was a thriving community of agricultural industries, as well as a mine. The *Black Venus* pub was once a row of Fortescue miners' cottages. In 1958 the Earl and Countess Fortescue died within days of each other, leaving the Challacombe estate crippled by death duties. A year later the village and 5,000 acres were sold at auction to an investment company, who sold it on to a private buyer, who sold most of the farms back to the tenants who had been out-bid in the first place.

Champflower   Huish Champflower is a small village in the wooded countryside overlooking the river Tone on the edge of the Brendon Hills in Somerset. A 'huish' was a measure of land that would support a family, from the Old English *hiwisc*. In 1274 the village was called Hywys Champflur after the Champflur family, lords of the manor in the 13th century.

Cheriton   Cheriton village is close to the beauty spot of Watersmeet. Cheriton Ridge, rising from the village, carries the Two Moors Way, a footpath linking Exmoor to Dartmoor, and the Tarka Trail. Named after *Tarka the Otter*, Henry Williamson's book, the trail follows, as far as possible, the route Tarka took along the rivers Taw and Torridge, 180 miles from Exmoor to Dartmoor.

Cloutsham   The village of Cloutsham lies at the foot of Dunkery Beacon and offers some of the best woodland walks on Exmoor. Overlooking Cloutsham Woods is Cloutsham Farm, which was once a hunting lodge of the Acland family.

Combe Martin   Combe Martin, on the north Devon coast, is said to have the longest village street in England. It also has a very long history, evident from the medieval strip fields, sunken lanes cut into the sides of the valley and the remains of former silver-mines. The 17th-century pub, the *Pack O' Cards*, was built from the winnings from a card game and has four storeys representing the four suits in the pack, 13 doors on each floor depicting the number of cards in each suit, and 52 windows, symbolising the number of cards in the pack.

Countisbury   Countisbury is a hilltop hamlet with only a church and an inn. Countisbury Hill plunges 1,000 feet in under two miles down from the moor into the middle of Lynmouth. The hill's main claim to fame is the part it played in the tale of 'The Overland Launch'. On the stormy night of 12 January 1899, when the seas were too rough to launch the lifeboat from Lynmouth, the men, women and horses from the village dragged and carried their lifeboat up the one-in-four gradient of Countisbury Hill, over the moor and down the even steeper and more tortuous Porlock Hill. Ten hours later, at 6.30 a.m. on Friday 13th, they managed to launch the lifeboat off Porlock Weir and went to the aid of the *Forest Hall*.

Croydon Close   Croydon Hill, about three miles south of Minehead, is said to be haunted. On dark and stormy nights can be heard the unearthly howls of the Devil of Croydon Hill in pursuit of an unfortunate butcher's boy. The tale goes that a ploughboy from Croydon village took his plough blade to be repaired at the smithy in nearby Rodhuish. While he was there, the butcher boy told him the tale of a devilish creature which haunted the hillside at night. Thinking it would be fun to scare the ploughboy, the butcher boy dressed up in a horned bull's hide and jumped out from behind a bush. The ploughboy struck out with his blade and ran home. The bull's hide with a gash in it was later found but the butcher boy was never seen again. The locals believed he was snatched by the Devil of Croydon Hill.

Danesbrook Close   The Danesbrook is one of the many rivers of Exmoor. Flanked by ancient Hollowcombe Woodlands, this fairly substantial and fast-flowing water eventually flows into the river Barle near Hawkridge. Deer, and the occasional glimpse of an otter, may be seen along its banks.

Dulverton Drive   Dulverton, Somerset, in the south of Exmoor, is a small but busy town. It stands where the deep Barle Valley opens out into meadowland before joining the river Exe. A medieval bridge crosses the river where the old workhouse now serves as the offices of the Exmoor National Park Authority.

Dunkery Beacon   Dunkery Beacon is the highest point on Exmoor, rising to 1,704 feet above sea level. There are magnificent views from the bracken and heather-clad slopes to the sea at Porlock Bay, and to a chain of summits which are capped with Bronze-Age barrows. Once the site of a fire beacon, a bonfire is still lit there when there is an important occasion to celebrate.

Dunster Court   Dunster is a much photographed Somerset market town with a broad main street flanked by old shops, tea-rooms and cottages and overlooked by the solid Norman castle. Central to this medieval tableau is the octagonal Yarn Market, preserved as a reminder of Dunster's days as a wool centre.

Elmhurst Close   Elmhurst village in Somerset is on the outskirts of Street, which is the home of Clark's shoe factory.

Exbridge   Exbridge on the southern fringe of Exmoor National Park, near Dulverton, has the rivers Exe and Barle running through it. It is a small, quiet, picturesque village, popular with canoeists, anglers, campers and walkers.

Exmoor Gate   This represents the gateway to Exmoor, one of England's most beautiful National Parks, which man has inhabited over 8,000 years. The remains of settlements, standing stones, burial mounds, field strips, and the relics of other ages are everywhere. The native Exmoor ponies still roam with the red deer, trout and otters play in the streams, and the wild moor and valleys are haunted by the dark romance of the Doones.

Favell Drive   The road names in the south-east corner of Furzton appear to illustrate the agricultural history of the land here, while also having relevance to the similar landscape of Exmoor. Favell and Braybrooke Drives run parallel and echo the names of the Northamptonshire villages of Weston Favell and Braybrooke. The connection may be that, in the early 19th century, these furze lands were used as 'fattening lands' to graze young steers for the Northamptonshire leather industry. Hugo Fauvell held the manor of Weston Feival in 1235, the family name evolving over the

Lakeside housing at Furzton.

years from Feival to Fauvel, Fauvell, Fauwell and, eventually, Favell by 1614.

Grasscroft   Probably reflects previous usage of this land. The fields surrounding farms and villages on Exmoor are integral features of its character. As sheep farming is predominant, many of the fields are grassland. Probably named to suggest a small piece of arable land left to grass.

Hawkridge   A small, pretty village in the south of Exmoor, Hawkridge lies below Tarr Steps, which is a long, low 'clapper' bridge made of stone slabs resting on one another across the river Barle. Its age is unknown, but it has been restored several times following flood damage. Hawkridge brook flows into the river Taw north of Umberleigh.

Holme Wood   Possibly refers to Holme Moor, in the Minehead area of Somerset, where the broad-leaved, deciduous Holme Wood covers 85 per cent of the moor, the rest consisting of grassland, bogs and marshes.

Hurlstone Grove   Hurlstone (or more correctly Hurtstone) Point juts off the Exmoor Heritage coastline near Selworthy Beacon and is reached by the south-west coast path from Minehead. There is an old coastguard look-out from which to view the bird life around the Bristol Channel.

Kingsbridge   Kingsbridge is a hamlet by a stream with an inn and pretty cottages sheltered by woodlands in the Brendon Hills.

Loxbeare Drive   Loxbeare is a small, scattered village in mid-Devon between Tiverton and South Molton. It is mentioned in Domesday Book as having been in the ownership of Drogo, a Norman baron who seems to have owned most of Devon in the later 11th century. Little seems to have changed there since.

Luccombe   Luccombe, in the Porlock area of Somerset, is a picturesque National Trust village with old cottages, a thatched shop and a beautiful church.

Luxborough Grove   Luxborough is a tiny, pastoral village in the Brendon Hills of Somerset. This is farming country, with green fields covering the rolling hillsides. A stream runs beside the lane through the village which consists of cottages and barns behind high hedgerows.

Lynmouth Crescent   Probably the most famous village in Devon, Lynmouth nestles on the coast at the mouth of the East and West Lynn rivers. In 1952 it was the scene of the Lynmouth Flood Disaster when, following prolonged rain, water from the moors above turned the Lynn rivers into a mighty torrent which swept away much of the village and claimed many lives. Although sympathetically restored, with a necessary accent on flood safety measures, some of the quaintness of old Lynmouth was lost for ever.

Marwood Close   Marwood village and Hill Gardens are about three miles north of Barnstaple. The gardens cover a 20-acre site in a landscaped woodland valley and are internationally famous for their collection of astilbes. Camellias, azaleas and rhododendrons put on a great show in season. There is also a bog garden and three small lakes containing enormous koi carp.

Medeswell   On an 1885 map of Bletchley, a well is marked in the north-west corner of the area known as Coldharbour. This may have been Medes well, *mede* or *mead* being an old word for a meadow.

Morebath Grove   Morebath is a small village about two miles from Bampton in mid-Devon, on the edge of Exmoor, with the rivers Exe and Barle close by. Its Victorian church is a replacement for a much earlier one which was deliberately gutted by fire in 1549, after the villagers joined in the West Country Prayer Book Rebellion against Henry VIII's Reformation. The then Catholic priest of Morebath, Sir Christopher Trychay, kept all the accounts of the parish meetings, vividly recording the activities of the villagers at this time.

Muddiford Lane   Muddiford is a village in a wooded combe by a river, about four miles from Barnstaple. Contrary to the seemingly obvious, this is not a place on a muddy ford. According to *The Oxford Dictionary of English Place-Names*, in 1303 the village was called 'Modeworthi', probably denoting a man called 'Moda', with the addition of *worthig,* Old English for 'enclosure', which at some time was replaced by 'ford', meaning a river-crossing.

Nettlecombe   Nettlecombe Court is a Tudor country mansion with its own little church nestling in a wooded valley in the Brendon Hills of west Somerset, just within the Exmoor National Park. Nettlecombe has been owned by the Wolseley family since the Norman era, but since 1968 the mansion has been let to the Leonard Wills Field Centre, which runs courses in ecology, geography fieldwork, environmental studies and natural history.

Northleigh Northleigh is a small village off the beaten track about three miles north of Barnstaple.

Oakridge Oakridge is the name of a farm on the moor above Ilfracombe.

Parkside Leading to the Furzton local park, this name also alludes to Exmoor National Park. National Parks were first established in 1949 for the purpose of maintaining valuable areas of the countryside in their natural state. Exmoor National Park, which covers 267 square miles, was designated in 1954. Exmoor National Park Authority is the organisation charged by central government to carry out the policies and legislation applicable to National Parks.

Perracombe This is a mis-spelling of the village of Parracombe, which nestles in a combe on the river Heddon, off the road to Lynton. The ancient church of the Celtic Saint Petrock is redundant now, but was saved from destruction by John Ruskin in 1878, when the new church was built. Its 18th-century interior is well preserved.

Pinkworthy Pinkworthy Pond (pronounced Pinkery by the locals) is a man-made lake in the middle of Exmoor. It was constructed in 1830 by landowner John Knight who, according to folktale, was a wealthy outsider from Worcestershire who thought he could transform this boggy part of Exmoor Forest into productive agricultural land. The lake may have been part of his drainage scheme, but the project was abandoned and nobody knows the real reason for the existence of Pinkworthy Pond. It dams the headwaters of the river Barle above Simonsbath.

Porlock Lane Porlock is renowned as the prettiest village in Somerset. With Exmoor rising on three sides behind it, the village is tucked in a combe beside the Bristol Channel. The quaint, historic harbour of Porlock Weir fingers out into the sea to the west and the alarmingly steep Porlock Hill twists and writhes its way up to the moor where red deer, sheep and ponies roam free. The poet Robert Southey stayed at Porlock's *Ship Inn* in 1798 and wrote a sonnet about the village as he sat by the fire. His fellow poets Wordsworth and Coleridge also visited Porlock and it was while staying at a nearby farm that Coleridge wrote his *Kubla Khan,* which he never finished, claiming that 'a man from Porlock' had called and shattered his inspiration.

Radworthy North Radworthy and South Radworthy are tiny hamlets a few miles apart on each side of the river Mole, with Radworthy Down between them and North Molton. Another Radworthy lies several miles north-west up on Challacombe Common. Above the reservoir, which was constructed in 1937, there is a deserted medieval village and site of a Celtic settlement where evidence of the distant past is everywhere: there are Bronze-Age field workings, Saxon earthworks, shards of properties, barrows and arcane standing stones.

Redhuish Close   This is a variation of Rodhuish, a village in the same area as Carhampton, Croydon and Bilbrook between the Brendon Hills and the Bristol Channel. A 'huish' was 'a measure of land that would support a family'.

Ryecroft   In the south-east corner of Furzton, this reflects previous use of the land. A croft is a small piece of arable land adjoining a farm, in this case a place where rye was grown.

Selworthy   Selworthy is a pretty village at the foot of Selworthy Beacon, Somerset. Known for its thatched cottages, which are owned by the National Trust, it has a white-washed church overlooking the green. From Selworthy Beacon there are magnificent views across Porlock Vale and along the coast.

Shallowford Grove   Shallowford consists of a handful of houses beside the babbling Barbrook in the depths of Exmoor. It can be reached by a very narrow lane, or by footpath, from Barbrook village behind Lynmouth. From Shallowford, a footpath climbs up and over Ilkerton Ridge to Furzehill. This is an area of Exmoor where free-living Exmoor ponies roam at will and megalithic sites are abundant.

Shirwell Crescent   Shirwell, an Exmoor village, lies in a combe between Barnstaple and Lynton. Its history revolves around the Chichester family, who owned the village, and Youlston Manor, where they lived until about 1919. There is a Methodist chapel, built in 1903 by the local farmers, and Shamefaced Lane is so called because it was a notorious lovers' lane.

Simonsbath   Simonsbath, in the Barle valley a few miles inland from Lynmouth, has been at the centre of the Royal Forest of Exmoor since Norman times, but the village of today was mostly built in the 19th century by John Knight after he bought this corner of the moor from the Crown. There is a pub, shop and tea-rooms popular with walkers and anglers.

Swimbridge Lane   Swimbridge is off the main road about four miles from Barnstaple, Devon. The local pub is called the *The Jack Russell* after Parson John (Jack) Russell, who was vicar of St James' church here from 1832 to 1883. When he arrived in Swimbridge, he had with him a small terrier called Trump, which he had acquired from the milkman when he was a student at college. He was so impressed with the little dog that he decided to breed from him, and so was born the Parson Jack Russell Terrier. While he was parson, he started restoration work on the church and there is a stained-glass window in his memory. Jack Russell's grave is in the churchyard and the dog depicted on the pub sign is Trump.

The Hedgerows The hedgerows along the lanes and round the fields are important features of the Exmoor landscape. They provide shelter for small mammals and birds.

Timberscombe Timberscombe is a village in a valley in the Exmoor National Park, about two miles from Dunster. This name derives from the obvious: 'valley where timber is obtained'. The village stands on the old turnpike road from Dunster to Dulverton and has several old cottages and an ancient church with a tower, rebuilt in 1714.

Treborough Treborough is a hamlet with a church and a handful of cottages, set deep in the Brendon Hills, off the A39.

Trentishoe Crescent Trentishoe is a small, picturesque village on the coastal path between Lynton and Combe Martin. Truly off the beaten path, the single-track lanes weave and dip between high hedges, the grass is tough and the trees bowed by the wind. The Old Farmhouse, at least 300 years old, was once the home of smugglers, and has connections with the Blackmore family who lived in Trentishoe from 1500. R.D. Blackmore, author of *Lorna Doone,* chose Trentishoe as the setting for his first novel, *Clara Vaughan.* Trentishoe Manor lies at the foot of Trentishoe Down, on top of which there is a tumulus, or ancient burial mound.

Twitchen Lane The name Twitchen comes from the Old English word *twicen(e),* meaning 'crossroads'. The village of Twitchen is set high on the southern edge of Exmoor at a once important crossroads. It is a remote and pretty hamlet with old cottages and a little church looking down a deep, wooded valley. Twitchen Ridge is above it, up on the moor, and Twitchen Mill lies to the south.

Washfield Washfield is a small village in the Exe Valley north-west of Tiverton and off the A361. In the same area as Calverleigh and Loxbeare, the name probably means 'open land near a place used for washing (sheep or clothes)', from the Old English *waesce* and *feld.*

Watchet Court Watchet is an old harbour town on the coast of Somerset and the edge of Exmoor. The poet Samuel Taylor Coleridge chose Watchet as the port from which his *Ancient Mariner* would 'set out on his fateful voyage', as he told his friend William Wordsworth. The harbour was commercially active until a few years ago, but now is used mostly by yachts and pleasure craft. The boat museum is by the harbour and the West Somerset light railway runs from Watchet station to Minehead.

Watersmeet Close Watersmeet is a well-known beauty spot in the steep wooded valleys of the East Lynn river and Hoare Oak Water, which run into each other here. The rivers tumble over rocks and boulders, through deep, wooded gorges, crossed at intervals by stone bridges. The 1,000-acre estate is owned by the National Trust and a 19th-century fishing lodge is now a visitors centre and tea garden.

Winsford Hill Winsford Hill, north-west of Dulverton, is a heath-covered common managed by the National Trust. At the highest point of the hill there are three Bronze-Age barrows. Winsford, with its thatched cottages and several bridges, including a packhorse bridge, over the Winn Brook and river Exe, has been called the prettiest village on Exmoor.

Wistmans   The only Wistmans found is Wistmans Wood on Dartmoor. This is a strange and twisted ancient woodland, said to be haunted by a pack of jet black Wish hounds or Yell hounds as they are also called. These are the ghostly hounds of the Midnight Hunter that hunts on Dartmoor on moonless nights. His horse breathes fire and flame and anyone who hears the baying of the hounds can expect to die within the year. Their favourite hunting ground is said to be along the ancient track called the Abbot's Way which runs near Wistmans Wood. English Nature are working to preserve this ancient oak woodland.

Withycombe   Withycombe is a small village on the Devon-Somerset border, at the edge of Exmoor National Park. In the old hundred of Carhampton, it is mainly a farming village with a stream running through it, a church dating from the 13th century, cottages and an old watermill which has been converted into a house.

KNOWLHILL

Knowlhill was the existing name of a field shown east of Loughton Manor on Ordnance Survey 153, map of Loughton dated 1769.

THEME On the other side of Watling Street opposite Shenley Lodge, Knowlhill continues the theme of Scientists and Inventors in the Field of Energy

Davy Avenue   Sir Humphrey Davy (1778-1829) was an English chemist and inventor, best known for his Davy safety lamp for miners, invented in 1815 and still used today. He also discovered the anaesthetic properties of nitrous oxide (laughing gas), the fact that chlorine is an element and that diamonds are a form of carbon. In 1807 he discovered potassium, then new metals of sodium, barium, strontium, calcium and magnesium. Davy was knighted in 1812 and elected President of the Royal Society in 1820.

Garforth Close   W.E. Garforth was a late 19th-/early 20th-century colliery engineer who developed mining equipment in the west Yorkshire coalfields. The Garforth GR6S flame safety lamp, which detects methane and firedamp, is used in mines all over the world and is incorporated in the Olympic flame.

Harrison Close   John Harrison (1693-1776) was the English inventor of the chronometer which determined longitude. He also invented the gridiron pendulum, the going fusee and the remontoir escapement. He invented a portable timekeeper with which mariners were able to work out their exact position on the high seas. After 50 years of trials and frustration, Harrison won the Board of Longitude's prize for his timepiece, the first clock able to withstand the rigours of the movement of the seas.

Kelvin Drive   William Thomson, 1st Baron Kelvin of Large (1824-1907), was a British physicist, mathematician and inventor. He made some astonishing discoveries and patented a large number of mechanical and electrical devices. He invented the household electricity meter, safety circuit fuses, and dynamo and electric machines. He put forward the idea of an absolute measurement of temperature, now known as the Kelvin scale, and established the law of the conservation of energy, as proposed by Joule. He discovered the Thomson effect of thermo-electricity and was knighted for his work on the electrical properties of cables which led to the laying of the first transatlantic cable in 1866.

Roebuck Way   Dr John Roebuck was an English inventor. He graduated as an MD, but gave up medical practice to do chemistry research. This led to improvements in methods of refining precious metals and in the production of chemicals. He developed the lead-chamber process of manufacturing acid from common salt. In 1759 he founded the Carron Iron Works in Stirlingshire and, later, was a friend and patron of James Watt, becoming his partner in the development of the steam engine, until he went bankrupt in 1773 and was replaced by Matthew Boulton.

Milton Keynes is Britain's most energy efficient city. Spectrum is a high-tech, energy efficient office and distribution centre in the heart of the city's 300-acre Energy Park, a unique residential and commercial development.

LOUGHTON

Loughton is one of the 13 villages already existing in the Milton Keynes designated area. Recorded in Domesday Book of 1086 as Lochintone, *the Old English name means 'estate associated with a man called Luhha'. The village was described in 1847 as being almost opposite the 49th milestone from London on the ancient Roman road called Watling Street. Two parishes and two manors, Great and Little Loughton, once co-existed, each with its own lord and rector, until the parishes were combined under Henry IV in about 1408.*

THEME **Parish History**

All Saints View   Self-explanatory, a road with a view of All Saints' church.

Ardys Court   The Ardys or Ardres family were lords of Great Loughton manor from about 1350 until 1415, when, on the marriage of an Ardys widow, or heiress, it passed to the Rushly family.

Ashpole Furlong   This name already existed as the name of a field.

All Saints' church, Loughton dates from the 15th century.

Bignell Croft   Frederic Wills Bignell was a Loughton benefactor. In his will he bequeathed money, stocks and dividends in trust for the needy of the village. He stipulated that on Christmas Eve money was to be distributed among the occupants of the four memorial cottages on London Road.

Bradwell Road   This is the old Bradwell road which still runs (with a few diversions) from Watling Street, through Loughton, to Bradwell.

Catesby Croft   Possibly an earlier relative of the 'Gunpowder Plot' Catesbys of nearby Ashby St Ledgers, Francis Catesby married Philippa, the widow of Jakes Edy, after he died in 1493. By his will, Philippa had inherited Little Loughton manor, but soon after her marriage to Catesby she died and the manor passed to John and Isabel Piggot. In 1544 Francis Catesby acquired the manor of Hardmead, near Newport Pagnell, where his family remained until 1675. There are memorials to the Catesbys in Hardmead. The family was also related by marriage to the Treshams.

Cavendish Court   Alice and Thomas Cavendish owned a quarter of Loughton manor before Thomas died in possession of it in 1524. He was succeeded by his son, George Cavendish.

Church Close   From where a footpath leads to the church of All Saints.

Church Lane   The existing name for the lane leading to the church.

Clover Close   Named after a field on which clover grew, and marked on the 1769 map of Loughton.

Common Lane   The old lane which leads up to and over Bradwell Common.

Cottage Common   Cottage Close and The Cottagers Close are field names marked on a 1769 map of Loughton. Cottages have stood here for many years.

Crane Court   The Crane family were lords of Loughton manor during the early 1600s and there are memorials to them in the church of All Saints. Before coming to Loughton, John Crane had served Elizabeth I and James I and was Chief Clerk of His Majesty's Kitchen, Officer of the Admiralty and Surveyor of all Victuals for Ships. In 1613 the Cranes bought Little Loughton manor from the Pigotts. They fought on the Royalist side during the Civil Wars, and in 1646 John Crane was heavily fined for delinquency (omitting to do his duty as Parliament required). In 1655 he sold the manor to Ralph Holt in order to pay off the last of his fine. He was the husband of Mary Tresham and father of their 16 children.

Ebbs Grove   Ebbs is a family name, long associated with Loughton.

Edy Court   The Edy family became lords of the manor of Little Loughton in about 1467. John Edy was regarded as a colourful but rather pompous and self-important man, who described himself as a squire, or gentleman. He sold Loughton manor to Richard Rivers and in 1487 bought the Mallets estate in Stony Stratford.

Loughton Manor Farm cottages dating from the late 16th or early 17th century.

Farnell Court   James Farnell held the rights to fisheries at Loughton Brook, together with lands and messuages, up to his death in January 1604. The properties passed to his son, John Farnell, who died on 28 September 1624, leaving three daughters as heirs. Ninety years later, at Easter 1714, the records for Buckinghamshire Sessions tell us that Griffin Farnell of the *Shenley Inn*, Loughton was 'a poor insolvent prisoner for debt, admitted to have his share of County Bread upon petition'. In 1784, a T. Farnell appears as tenant of a freehold property at Loughton belonging to John Griffith of Moulsoe.

Loughton Brook near The Green, Loughton.

Glebe Close   The Glebe Farm once stood here, and The Glebe was also the name given to the Rectory House. A very old name, glebe is the land attached to a parish church.

Greenhill Close   'Green Hill Furlong' was the name of a field shown on the Inclosure Map of Loughton 1769.

Gurney Close   Gurney is an old village family name. Several of them are buried in the graveyard of All Saints' church. In 1377-82, John Gerneys was rector of the church at Great Loughton.

Higgs Court   John Higgs was a local blacksmith. Albert Ernest Higgs ran *The Bell Inn* during the 19th century.

Hillcrest Close   According to *Kelly's Directory* of 1931 and 1939, a Mrs Hillcrest lived in London Road, Loughton at that time. Also, a house named Hill Crest is believed to have existed here in the early 1950s.

Holm Gate   This is the gateway road into Loughton, opposite Great Holm.

Holt Grove   The Holt family were lords of the manor from 1655, when they bought it from the Cranes. More than a hundred years later, on 1 March 1766, Ralph Holt was supposed to be entertaining the Rev. William Cole, diarist, of Bletchley to dinner, but had to cancel because his tenant's wife, Mrs Yorke, had eaten hemlock roots instead of parsnip and died. Six other members of the Yorke family who had also eaten the poison were very ill.

Homestall Place   The Homestall was the name of a field, listed in a 1710 record of Loughton lands. A homestall is another word for a homestead. A homestead/homestall moat was a moated house and in Norman times they could be found in every parish where there was a stream, or clay soil. A farm or manor house was built on a mound up to 30 feet high by digging out a moat up to eight feet deep to create a mini fortress within which to keep farm animals and buildings. At Little Loughton there was a homestead moat which was levelled in 1945.

Homeward Court   'Homeward Coombs' was the name of a field owned by Richard Sumner and shown on a 1769 map of Loughton.

Hoppers Meadow   The Hopper family were lords of the manor between the Lucys and the Cranes in the 15th century.

Hugh Parke Close   Hugh Parke was rector of All Saints' church, Loughton from 1485 to 1514. There is a memorial to him in the church.

Hutchings Close   'Hutchings Furlong' was the name of a field, shown on the 1769 map of Loughton.

Kirkham Court   The Kirkham family possessed the manor of Shenley in the late 14th and early 15th centuries.

Knowl Gate   The road opposite Knowl Hill leading into Loughton. Knowle Hill is recorded in 1769 as the name of a field lying on this site.

Leys Road   Leys are arable land, or pasture.

Linceslade Grove   'Linceslade Common', 'Lyneslade Furlong' and 'Limslade Closes' were all fields marked on the 1769 map of Loughton as belonging to Thomas Turville.

Little Meadow   The name of the field on which these houses were built.

London Road   This is a length of the old London road, or Watling Street, which passed through the village before a new stretch was built to bypass it at this point in the 1970s.

Lucy Lane   The Lucy family held the manor of Loughton during the 16th century.

Loughton Lodge   Named after Lodge Farm shown on Ordnance Survey map 116.

Old Bell Lane   Commemorates *The Bell Inn*, which was one of Loughton's several public houses until it was demolished in 1948.

Paynes Drive   Paynes Close was the name of a field in Little Loughton, shown on a 1769 map. It was possibly occupied by a forefather of the Payne family who lived at number 35 Bletchley Road from about 1882 to 1900. In 1911, number 35 was bought by the Co-op and in 1941, when the water supply pipe was being renewed, a workman named Charles Dickens unearthed a tin containing gold and silver coins and jewellery, including a gold watch inscribed 'G.F. Payne, Bedford, 1862'. As no Payne relatives

Above: horses grazing in paddocks in School Lane, Loughton. Right: Elm House.

could be traced, Charles Dickens was awarded 75 per cent of the treasure trove.

Pinks Close   This was the name of a field, possibly tenanted by a farmer called Pink.

Pitcher Lane   This lane is marked on old maps and is said to have been so named because the villagers drew their water from the well here, carrying it home in pitchers.

Redland Drive   'Redland Close' and 'Redland Furlong' were the names of two fields, shown on the 1769 map of Loughton.

Rushleys Close   This refers to the family of Rushley, who were lords of the Little Loughton, or Ardres manor, after Alan Rushley of Turvey in Bedfordshire acquired the rights in 1371. In 1395 Ardres manor passed to the Lucy family.

School Lane   The lane which once led to the old National School, built in 1867 for the 70 local children.

Snaith Crescent   Arthur Snaith was a popular headmaster and local councillor in the 1970s. He led the opposition to the proposed building of the new city, calling it 'a hearse for North Bucks'. He led the North Bucks Association of the 12 rural parishes who had decided to fight the new city, and was its secretary.

Specklands   This was the name of an ancient track and field, marked on a 1769 map of Loughton.

Sumner Court   Mr Richard Sumner was a landowner in Loughton in 1769, shown on the Inclosure Map of Loughton as owning 'Sumner Well Common' and 'Homeward Coombs'.

The Green   This is a short lane which leads across Loughton Brook to the old village green which was at the heart of the old village. A conservation area, there are several listed farm cottages spaced around the green, the site of Little Loughton Manor which was remodelled in 1580 by Valentine Pigott. Parts of the house were built in 1500 or earlier.

The Meadow   Named after a field which was once a meadow.

Thorwold Place   A house called Thorwold once stood here. The name is possibly a corruption of the name 'Vorwelleslade', meaning 'meadow before the well by the stream', which was the name of a field in medieval Loughton. Or it may be an amalgamation of that name with 'Tholdestrete', meaning ' the old street' and recorded as an old Loughton name, or 'Thohidemede'.

Tresham Court   Mary Tresham was the wife of John Crane, lord of both the Loughton manors in the early 17th century and Chief Clerk of His Majesty's Kitchen and Officer of the Admiralty. Mary Tresham gave birth to 11 sons and five daughters. The Treshams were wealthy Catholic Northamptonshire landowners and Francis Tresham died as a prisoner in the Tower of London while awaiting trial for his conspiratorial role in the Gunpowder Plot. John Tresham had right of ownership of the Ardres manor in about 1625.

Turvill End   Thomas Turville owned a considerable amount of land at Loughton in 1769.

Wallmead Gardens   'Wall Mead Common' was the name of a field, shown on a 1769 map of Loughton.

Weldon Rise   The Reverend Mr Weldon Champnes held a portion of Loughton manor in 1769.

Whitworth Lane   Henry Billington Whitworth of Northampton inherited a share of the manor of Loughton from his father, Robert Whitworth of London, who died in 1832. He also owned a farm at Loughton, which he bought in 1848 from the estate of the late James Hill.

Wilmin Grove   Henry Wilmin was a local farmer. He sold one acre of a nine-acre field to Samuel Holman, who built a smock mill on it at Bradwell. In 1784, John Wilmin of Bradwell appears on the Poll for Knights of the Shire for the County of Buckingham, as a freeholder of property tenanted by W. Wilkinson.

Woodward Place   The name of Thomas Woodward of Loughton appears on a 1524 Subsidy Roll for the County of Buckinghamshire. Therefore, he appears to have been a landowner, obliged to pay tax on his possessions to King Henry VIII.

SHENLEY BROOK END

Shenley Brook End, called after the brook running through it, was anciently a small hamlet and one of three manors in the parish of Shenley. In the Middle Ages the Brook-end manor was held by the Beauchamps until 1397, when Thomas Beauchamp, Earl of Warwick was attainted (lost his civil rights through conviction for high treason), and it was granted to Thomas Mowbray, who became Duke of Norfolk. After 1426 it was held jointly with Church-end manor. Shenley brook still flows from the priory in Whaddon, through Shenley Brook End and across Milton Keynes before joining the Great Ouse river north of New Bradwell.

THEMES (1) Shenley Parish History
(2) Breeds of Livestock and Poultry

Alderney Place   For a short time at the turn of the 19th and 20th centuries, the Channel Island of Alderney managed to produce its own breed of cow. A hybrid of Jersey and Guernsey cattle, the first truly Alderney calf was distinguished by its intermediate size, reddish colour and individual white markings. The Channel Island breeds were already popular in America, and so many Alderneys were exported that demand outstripped supply. With mixed breeding programmes in America and the effects of world war on Alderney, the breed deteriorated and died out, the last true Alderney calf being born in 1927.

Alpine Croft   The Alpine goat, bred in the mountainous regions of Europe, was brought to Britain in the early 1900s and was developed into the British Alpine. Tall and rangy, it is a graceful goat with a black coat and white markings and a very good milk producer.

Ancona Gardens   A breed of poultry, the Ancona is a speckled variety of laying hen. Of Mediterranean descent, it is named after Ancona in Italy.

Angora Close   Angora was an earlier form of Ankara, now the capital of Turkey. The Angora goat which originated here was a prized possession and anybody caught exploiting or exporting them was punished by death. They have only been in England since 1982. In appearance very similar to a sheep, it has very long, fast-growing hair which forms into ringlets out of which mohair is made. There is also an Angora rabbit, probably so named because of its very long, silky hair which is only used in handcrafted work as it is not commercially viable. The Turkish Angora cat also originated in Turkey. Oriental in appearance, it has medium-length silky hair which is not used for anything.

Berkshire Green   The Berkshire is a breed of pig which originated around 1790 in the Thames Valley, was very popular in the 19th and early 20th centuries, but declined almost to extinction in the 1960s with the introduction of intensive farming methods. The modern Berkshire is a small, black pig with white nose, feet and tail tip and a placid disposition. The breed is kept alive by enthusiastic breeders with the support of the Rare Breeds Survival Trust.

Blackwell Place   Blackwell Furlong was a field name shown in the list of Shenley land enclosures of 1762.

Bletchley Road   This is a length of the old road which once ran from Bletchley to Shenley Brook End.

Braford Gardens   The Braford is a breed of cattle developed in America by Alto Adams, a Florida breeder, by crossing a herd of 7/8ths Braham and 1/8th Florid Scrub with Herefords.

Bremen Grove   This is possibly an adaptation of Brahman, the sacred cattle of India, named after the Hindu god Brahma. They are characterised by a hump over the shoulder and neck, a muscular appearance, large, pendulous ears, upswept horns and a large dewlap.

Brices Meadow   William Brice was a local tenant farmer. In John Knapp's plan and survey of his Shenley lands in 1771, Brice is shown as having a homestead and a holding of 12 fields and meadows.

Burdeleys Lane   William Burdeleys was rector of St Mary's church, Shenley for about three years from 1305 to 1308.

Bushey Bartrams   This is said to have been the name of a field here in the 16th century.

Calves Close   The name of a field where calves were kept in the 19th century and shown on an 1801 map of the Shenley estates and a tithe map of 1840.

Candy Lane   W.S. Candy was a local farmer who rented the pasture which was once on this ground.

Cashmere Close   The Cashmere, or Kashmiri, is a breed of small goat which has an undercoat of long, soft white hair, famously used for making the finest woollen garments and fabrics. Originating in the mountainous regions of Kashmir, it is now domesticated and bred also for its milk and meat.

Chalwell Ridge   Chalwell Ridge Way was the name of an old track running through the Shenley and Salden areas. Sir John Fortescue, who had built a mansion at Salden and bought the three Shenley manors in 1578, had a map drawn up in 1599 showing all his posessions, which included Chalwell Ridge Way and the fields round about it.

Charbray Crescent   The Charbray is a breed of cattle which was developed in the Rio Grande area of America by crossing Charolais cattle with the Brahman, the hump-backed Indo-Chinese Ox. The Charbray is a large, rugged, muscular breed with the characteristic loose skin and large dewlap of the Brahman, although the hump is less obvious. The calves are usually a tan colour when born but lighten to the creamy white Charolais colouring with maturity.

Chartley Court   Chartley Park, a few miles to the north-east of Stafford, is home to one of only four remaining herds of Old English White Park cattle. A truly ancient breed, and once known as White Forest cattle, in the 13th century several herds roamed Chartley and other parks across Britain. In 1905 the Chartley herd was dispersed, but it has been re-established in recent years. During the Second World War it was recognised that White Park cattle were a valuable part of British heritage and were becoming an endangered species. Some were 'evacuated' to America for safe keeping while other herds went to Woburn and Whipsnade.

Chillingham Court The Wild White Cattle of Chillingham Park, near Alnwick, Northumberland are descendants of the original White Park breed of ancient cattle which have roamed there for the past 700 years. Before the 13th century they roamed freely in the forest which stretched from the North Sea coast to the Clyde estuary, but when the King decided to enclose his Chillingham castle it is believed that the cattle were confined within the castle bounds to provide a source of food.

Church End Road   This is a stretch of the original country road which branched off to the right from Bletchley Road and wound its way to Shenley Church End.

Copes Haven   John Cope was granted Shenley's Westbury Manor for life by King Henry IV in 1403 after it had been forfeited by the previous owner.

Cranwell Close   Richard Cranwell was rector of St Mary's church, Shenley between 1456 and 1482, when he went to Upminster, Essex, exchanging incumbencies with John Garthwaite, who came to Shenley.

Cressey Avenue   George Cressey was rector of the church of St Mary, Shenley for 26 years, from 1657 until his death in 1683.

Curtis Croft   The Curtis family were local farmers. Curtis's Close was the name of a field rented by them in 1771 from John Clarke and shown on a plan and survey of enclosures drawn up by the then lord of the manor, John Knapp.

Dorking Place   The Dorking is a breed of table fowl. Named after Dorking in Surrey, it is said to be the descendant of birds imported by the Romans. It has five claws on each foot, variously coloured plumage and lays white eggs.

Egerton Gate   William Egerton was rector of St Mary's church, Shenley between 1644 and 1656.

Fossey Close   Henry Fossey was a tenant farmer in Shenley during the 18th century. On a plan and survey of Shenley lands drawn up in 1771 by the then lord of the manor, John Knapp, Fossey is listed as holding eight fields, including Shenley Wood, the Toot and moated island, Oakhill Woods and Shepherd's Spinney.

Garthwaite Crescent   John Garthwaite was rector of St Mary's church, Shenley for about two years from 1482-4.

Gayal Croft   The Gayal is a species of ox found in the mountainous regions of east India and Burma. It can be found roaming wild, but many of them have been semi-domesticated.

Hamburg Croft   The Hamburg is a handsome, ornamental fowl, now mainly bred for show. Although it has a German name, it is believed to have originated in Holland. The colour variety ranges from black through gold to an amazing pattern of spangled white, silver and black. They lay small, white-shelled eggs.

Harlequin Place   The Harlequin is a breed of wild sea duck which inhabits the northern regions of Canada, Alaska, Greenland, Iceland and Siberia. Of harlequined black, white, grey and brown colours, they are 15-21 inches long with a 26-inch wingspan and their smart, elegant appearance has earned them the nickname of 'lords and ladies'.

Hartdames   This is said to have been the name of a field here in the 16th century. English place-names with the prefix 'Hart' usually refer to the male deer, or stag, although sometimes it derives from the name of a person called Hart. Therefore this field may have been worked by the dames of the Hart family.

Islingbrook   This is said to have been the name of a field.

Landrace Court   The result of over fifty years of breeding in Scandinavia, the Landrace is probably the most familiar breed of pig. With its long back, good shoulders, white colour and forward-pitched ears, it produces good pork and bacon.

Little Stocking   This was the name of a field shown on an 1801 map of the Shenley lands held by the Selby estate. The Old English word *stoccing* meant a clearing where there were tree-stumps.

Magpie Close   Magpie ducks were first introduced as a breed in the 1920s in Wales. They can be either black and white or grey and white, are free rangers and keen swimmers and are bred both for their eggs and their meat. Each bird lays about 180 eggs a year.

Manifold Lane   Running through from Emerson Valley, this road is named after the Manifold river and valley in Derbyshire.

Maxham   Written as 'Moxon's' on John Knapp's 1771 plan and survey of his Shenley lands, this was the name of one of the fields farmed by William Brice.

Minorca Court   Named after the Spanish island, the Minorca is the largest of the Mediterranean breeds of fowl. It was developed to produce very large eggs with a chalk-white shell but is now bred mainly for exhibition. A strong-bodied bird with black, white or blue plumage, it has a long tail, a large red comb and wattle and white ear lobes. Minorcas were kept by T.E. Lawrence (Lawrence of Arabia).

Nether Grove   Refers to the Nether field which was enclosed by an Act of 1762.

Orpington Grove   The Orpington is a breed of poultry, first bred by William Cook in 1886 on his farm in Orpington, Kent. The first birds were Black and over the next few years the White and the Buff were bred. The Buff was then classified separately under its own breed club, the Buff Orpington Club. With the introduction of the Blue Orpington, there are now four varieties of these show birds, which come in both full and bantam size.

Oxhouse Court   This was probably farmland on which stood an oxhouse, or cattle barn.

Plantation Place   In 1927 there was a 167-acre woodland plantation here.

Prentice Grove   Prentice was the name of a local family.

Rosecombe Place   A rose-combe is a fowl's low noduled comb, found on the heads of some chickens. The Buff Rose-comb is the name given to a species of Leghorn chicken. It is a handsome bird with golden-buff plumage and a rose-coloured comb.

Stubbs Field   Stubbs field and Stubbs south field were the names of fields shown on John Knapp's 1771 plan and survey of enclosures at Shenley. They bordered Watling Street at Shenley Church End and were under the tenancy of Richard Newman.

Sultan Croft   Originating in Turkey, the Sultan is a variety of ornamental fowl with a very distinctive appearance. Bred strictly for show, it has a large crest, muffs and beard with extravagant feathering on the feet and legs.

Tacknell Drive   Tacknell was the name of a field marked on a map of the Selby estate, which included lands at Winslow, Whaddon, Tattenhoe and Shenley. Whaddon Hall was the family seat, and in the early 20th century William Selby owned Shenley's Westbury Manor. The name Tacknell may refer to the name of a tenant farmer, or possibly derives from a historical meaning. For instance, a *tack* is another word for a tenure or a lease, particularly in the Scottish Highlands.

The Ryding   A riding is a track, especially a woodland track, for riding along. Riding Close, marked on John Knapp's 1771 plan and survey, corresponds with where The Ryding is today. In 1771 it was one of Henry Fossey's holdings and there were other Ridings at Shenley Wood and Oakhill Wood.

Tompkins Close   Tompkins field is shown on a 1698 map of the area.

Upper Wood Close   Upper Wood Close was the original name of the field on which the houses in this road were built. It is marked on the plan and survey drawn up by John Knapp in 1771, when it was in the tenancy of John Billington.

Walbank Grove   Richard Walbank was appointed rector of Walton parish church in 1477 but, after eight years in the post, resigned in 1485 to become rector of St Mary's church, Shenley, where he served until 1508.

Wallinger Drive   Henry Wallinger was a local tenant of the Shenley estate in 1903.

Welsummer Grove   Welsummers are a Dutch breed of chicken which originated in Welsum, Holland and were first imported into England in 1928. They are good free-range foragers and lay large, dark-brown eggs. The hens have red and black plumage and the cocks are handsome golden-red, with black tail feathers and large red combs.

Whaddon Road   This is a stretch of the old road leading to Whaddon.

SHENLEY CHURCH END

Shenley Church End is the name of the village which existed before the arrival of Milton Keynes. The name derives from the Anglo-Saxon Scienan-leage, *meaning bright clearing.*

THEMES **(1) Local and Parish History, including Field Names (2) Medieval Castles**

Aldwycks Close   A field named Aldwick's Close and Spinney is shown on John Knapp's plan and survey of the Shenley lands in 1771, under the tenancy of farmer John Clarke.

Baily Court   Joseph Baily was an 18th-century rector of St Mary's church. Described as a 'chief proprietor of the parish of Shenley', his seat was Shenley House, an impressive stone mansion by the church.

Bateman Croft   Thomas Bateman was a local farmer.

Beaumaris Grove   Beaumaris Castle, Anglesey, North Wales was the last to be built by Edward I's architect, James of St George, and is regarded as the most technically perfect medieval castle in Britain. It commands the old ferry crossing point to Anglesey and is a World Heritage listed site.

Benbow Court   This is named after 'old Mr Benbow', a locally well-known wheelwright whose shop was on the eastern side of London Road at Loughton (the old route of Watling Street), roughly on the site of Benbow Court.

Blatherwick Court   Sir Humphrey de Blatherwyke, of Blatherwick in

Northamptonshire, was the legal heir to the manor of Tattenhoe, being a cousin of Thomas Stafford, who was childless. However, Stafford had an illegitimate son, William, to whom he wanted to leave the manor, but in 1515 Blatherwyke heard of the 'cunning plan', got hold of the deeds and sent them to Woburn Abbey for safe keeping. The bastard heir sued the Abbot for their recovery and was given the manor for his lifetime in return for a £10 rent to be paid to the legitimate Staffords.

Bodiam Close   Bodiam Castle, beside the River Rother in East Sussex, was originally a coastal defence, but in 1385 Sir Edward Dalyngrygge built a stone castle. It exemplifies the transition from traditional medieval stronghold to the more habitable style of fortified castle home. Surrounded by a wide moat, it has a cylindrical tower at each corner and rectangular towers between. It was badly gutted during the Civil War and left to decay until the 20th century, when Earl Curzon carried out a partial restoration.

Brough Close   Brough Castle in Cumbria was built about 1100 and destroyed by the Scots in 1174. Towards the end of the 12th century it was rebuilt and became the seat of the Clifford family until the late 1600s. They enlarged it over the years, but after a fire in 1521 it lay derelict until 1659-62, when Lady Anne Clifford restored it in pseudo-medieval style. Today it is a ruin protected by English Heritage.

Burchard Crescent   In the reign of Edward the Confessor, Burghard was a Saxon thane shown in Domesday Book as holding the manors of Shenley.

Cecily Court   Cecily was the daughter of Sir Edmund Ashfield, lord of the manor of Shenley in the mid-16th century. She was married to Sir John Fortescue, but she died in about 1570 having had three sons, Robert, Francis and William. More than a century earlier, another Cecily, wife of William Sydney, inherited Westbury Manor from her father, Nicholas Wolbergh.

Daubney Gate   Sir Giles Daubney purchased the manor of Shenley from Lord Grey de Wilton in 1505 and sold it in 1520 to the Pigotts.

Dudley Hill   William and Joseph Dudley were both farmers in Shenley, and Dudleys Close is shown on John Knapp's 1771 plan and survey of his Shenley lands. William is recorded as living in Shenley Brook End in 1642, and 'The Late Dudley's Close' is recorded as a field in an 18th-century survey of the lands of Loughton, Shenley and Tattenhoe. Also, on the castles theme, Dudley Castle, West Midlands was first built in 1071 and rebuilt in 1530 as a Renaissance palace for John Dudley, who was later beheaded by Mary Tudor for his part in the plot to put Lady Jane Grey on the throne. During the Civil Wars it was a Royalist stronghold, but surrendered in 1645 after Charles I was captured. It was lived in by the Earls of Dudley until 1750 when it was gutted by a fire which raged for three days.

Duncan Grove   Lt Col William Duncan, JP purchased a share of Shenley Park estate and Westbury Farm for his daughter, Mrs Richard Selby-Lowndes, who still owned it in 1927.

Edmund Court   This could be any one of a number of Edmunds connected with Shenley's long history. The Reverend Richard Edmunds LLB was rector of St Mary's church from 1574 until his death in 1604, aged 82. His gravestone is under the communion table. There were two other rectors of St Mary's church, Edmund Ward 1432-*c*.1440 and Edmund Lee 1568-73, who might qualify, as might Sir Edmund Ashfield, who was bailiff and steward of the courts of the manor in 1546 and held the manor in about 1563. He died in about 1577. There was also Edmund, son and heir of John, Lord Grey de Wilton who negotiated the sale of the manor to Hugh Dennis and Thomas Wolverston between 1506 and 1509.

Engaine Drive   Mentioned in Domesday Book, in 1086 Richard Engaine, or Ingania, held land at Shenley jointly with Earl Hugh of Chester and Urse de Bersers. Engaine's main manor was Benefield in Northamptonshire, to which was attached Westbury Manor at Shenley.

Fortescue Drive   Sir John Fortescue of Salden (see p.54) was a cousin and tutor of Queen Elizabeth I and her Chancellor of the Exchequer 1589 to 1603. In about 1565 he bought the manor of Salden near Mursley and built the mansion, Salden House, where he entertained the Queen. She made him Keeper of the Great Wardrobe and entrusted him with 'both the ornaments of my soul and body'. Sir John became MP for Buckinghamshire and was in Parliament for 40 years. Through his marriage to Cecily, daughter of Sir Edmund Ashfield, lord of the manor of Shenley, Sir John Fortescue succeeded to the Shenley estate upon Ashfield's death in about 1573. Thereafter, the manors of Salden and Shenley descended together in the Fortescue's ownership for the next 100 years. Salden House was demolished in 1738 and a remaining portion was converted into a farmhouse.

Framlingham Court   Framlingham Castle in Suffolk is a remarkably well-preserved 12th-century castle. With its 13 towers, it has been a fortress, an Elizabethan prison, a poor house and a school. It was originally built by Earl Roger Bigod in about 1190 and, shortly after its completion, was captured in 1215 by the forces of King John.

Francis Court   There are three men named Francis in Shenley's history: Francis Pigott who held the manor from 1520 until he died in 1552; Francis Ashfield, second son of Sir Edmund Ashfield who held the manor in the 1570s, and Francis Duncombe, who was rector of St Mary's church in 1629.

Gramwell   The family of Ralph de Gramewell lived at Shenley in about 1284.

Hedges Court   John Hedges was a local farmer. He lived at Shenley Grange in the early 20th century and was killed in a car crash in 1943, aged 84.

Hedingham Court   Hedingham Castle in Essex was built in about 1140

A shared ownership property in Shenley Church End. Shared ownership is an arrangement by which a purchaser can buy a percentage of the value of a private property and pay rent on the remainder.

by Aubrey de Vere, grandfather of Hugh de Vere, lord of the manor of Calverton. Aubrey was created 1st Earl of Oxford by Queen Matilda. Hedingham remained the seat of the rich and powerful de Veres for 550 years and is owned today by a descendant, the Hon. Thomas Lindsay.

Holy Thorn Lane   Named after the famous Glastonbury Thorn, the holy thorn is a very old white hawthorn tree which blooms in Shenley at Christmas time in honour of Christ's birth. According to the fable, in AD 63 Joseph of Arimathea brought the Christian faith and the Holy Grail to Glastonbury, and in this place his staff took root, budded and bloomed at Christmas time. Now a variety of hawthorn which flowers around Christmas Day is called the Glastonbury or Holy Thorn.

Jenkins Close   Jenkins Close was the name of a field shown on John Knapp's 1771 plan and survey of Shenley lands. Also shown is Jenkin's orchard and yard.

Kirke Close   There is a monument in the church to Anna Kirke, who died in 1428. Simultaneously, in the early 15th century the Kirkham family were granted the manor. After Anne Kirkham died in 1427 it passed to John Kirkham of Shenley in 1435.

Knapp Gate   The Knapp family of Shenley and Little Linford came to the area in 1684. John Knapp was a City lace merchant who bought the manor of Little Linford and, three years later, one of the Shenley manors. The family provided Sheriffs in 1767 and 1858 and Justices of the Peace in every generation. Matthew Knapp was rector of the parish 1709-52 and Primatt Knapp from 1755 to 1792. Primatt was still lord of the manor in 1806 and the title remained in the Knapp family until the beginning of the 20th century. In 1905 they bought the manor of Newport (Pagnell).

Launceston Court   Launceston Castle, Cornwall is set on the motte of an original Norman castle. Towering above the town and countryside around Launceston, it defended the main route into Cornwall. Of the medieval castle, the tower and shell keep still survive.

Lipscomb Lane   George Lipscomb, an early 19th-century Buckinghamshire historian, wrote in 1820 of the almshouses built at Shenley Church End in 1615 at the behest of Sir Thomas Stafford, lord of the manor of Tattenhoe. In his will Stafford had requested that an almshouse or hospital be built for the benefit of six poor people, four men and two women. In 1847 George Lipscomb's *The History and Antiquities of Buckinghamshire* was published in several volumes.

Lowndes Grove   William Lowndes was a close friend of Thomas James Selby. When Selby died in 1772 he bequeathed his property at Tattenhoe and Westbury to Lowndes, together with the manors of Whaddon and Nash. Lowndes changed his name to Selby-Lowndes in 1783. In 1801 he had maps made of the area, one of which includes Westbury, Tattenhoe and Shenley Common. From 1813 to 1827 Richard Lowndes was minister of St Giles' church, Tattenhoe. Other members of the Lowndes family were Robert Lowndes of Great Brickhill, who kept a pack of harriers (hare hounds), and his nephew William Lowndes of Winslow, who was the great-grandson of William Lowndes, Queen Anne's Secretary to the Treasury. Descendants of the Selby-Lowndes family still live in the Milton Keynes area.

Mansell Close   The Maunsell, or Mansel, family held all Shenley from about 1190 when Thomas Maunsell was lord of the manor. By 1250 his son Thomas had succeeded him and supported Simon de Montfort against Henry III. By the end of the 13th century, he had given about 200 acres of Shenley lands to Woburn Abbey. In 1276 John de Grey, on behalf of Edward I, seized Shenley Manor, but he misappropriated it (sold off part for his own gain) and the king confiscated it and gave it to William de Ayet. From 1223-8 William Mansel was rector of St Mary's church. The manor of Shenley Brook End was once known as Shenley-Mansell.

Matilda Gardens   Matilda of Flanders was William the Conqueror's queen. Matilda was a popular name in the 11th and 12th centuries. Here it most likely refers to a co-heiress of the Maunsell or Mansel family who married Richard de la Vache. Another Matilda was the wife of Warin de Tatehoe (Tattenhoe) who, in about 1250, 'for the salvation of his soul and that of his wife, Matilda, granted to Snelshall priory his dyke [*fossa*] which lies below his courtyard between the land of the Prior of Snelshall in length and the green of Tatehoe and it extends towards Westcroft'. In 1272 Warinus was the Prior of Snelshall.

Matthew Court   Matthew Knapp was lord of Shenley Brook End manor in the 19th century. In the 1820s he was a Captain in the Bucks Hussars. He sold the manor in 1868 to Charles Morrell. Earlier, 1709-53, another

Matthew Knapp was rector of St Mary's church and, earlier still, Matthew de la Vache, son of Richard de la Vache, succeeded to Shenley manor in about 1316.

Morrell Close   Charles Morrell bought the manor of Shenley in 1868 from Matthew Knapp.

Musgrove Place   Fields known as Musgrove land are shown on a 1656 survey map.

Nathanial Close   This refers to Nathaniel Knapp, a nephew of Matthew Knapp. In 1778 he succeeded to the manors in Shenley and Linford. He never married and, after his death in 1795, his property passed to the Reverend Primatt Knapp, who was rector of St Mary's church, Shenley.

Oakhill Close   The name is taken from Oakhill Wood, which lies to the north of the medieval royal hunting forest of Whaddon Chase. The wood dates from pre-1086. A field named Oakhill Close, and Oakhill Lane, are shown on John Knapp's plan and survey of 1771 as tenanted by John Sibthorp.

Oakhill Road   For most of its length this road remains a country lane. On a 1983 Milton Keynes Development Corporation map of the area's heritage sites, taken from old Ordnance Survey maps, Oakhill Road is shown as a medieval trackway called Green Lane. In the 16th century, Oakhill was an area of land of 16 acres in Shenley Church End. It was described as 'of woods well sett with young oke' and is shown on John Knapp's 1771 plan and survey as Oakhill Wood north and south under the tenancy of Henry Fosseye. Running from Oakhill through Shenley Church End, Loughton, Bradwell and on to Haversham Mill is the ancient trackway, Swans Way, now a bridlepath.

Orford Court   Orford Castle, Woodbridge, Suffolk is a 12th-century royal castle built by Henry II as a coastal defence to protect the port of Orford and, it is said, to impress Hugh Bigod, a powerful earl with four castles in East Anglia. Overlooking Orford Ness, it has three huge towers and a magnificent keep which still survive. In its day it was regarded as a marvel of modern design.

Oville Court   William de Oville was rector of St Mary's church, Shenley from 1229 to 1241.

Peers Lane   Several members of the peerage have owned Shenley over the centuries. One of the manorial families was actually named Peers.

Phillip Court   This possibly refers to Thomas Phillips, a principal landowner in Whaddon. Alternatively, Sir Philip de la Vache inherited the manor from his father, Richard de la Vache, in 1377 and represented Buckinghamshire in Parliament. Also, Philip Fitz-Eustace owned land in Shenley in 1398. He was the son and heir to John Fitz-Eustace who inherited the Westbury Manor from his father in 1385.

Pigott Drive   The Pigott family were north Buckinghamshire landowners who held several manors during the 15th and 16th centuries. Their main seat was at Whaddon, which was part of Jane Seymour's dowry when she married Henry VIII, and was afterwards given to the Pigotts. In Whaddon church there is a monument to Thomas Pigott, Sarjeant at Law, who died in 1519. Francis Pigott held the manor of Shenley during the first half of the 16th century until his death in 1552. The Pigotts also owned Little Loughton Manor.

Pleshey Close   Pleshey Castle, five miles north of Chelmsford, Essex, is a 12th-century motte and bailey castle with extensive outer walls and earthworks. It was originally owned by the Mandeville family. Geoffrey de Mandeville, Earl of Essex, was Constable of the Tower in about 1130 but was a traitor, first to King Stephen and then to Empress Matilda. The Mandeville family were lords of the manor of Stoke Mandeville, Buckinghamshire in the 13th century. Most of Pleshey Castle was pulled down in 1629 for building materials. It is mentioned in Shakespeare's *Richard II.*

Rayleigh Close   Only the ruins of Rayleigh Castle in Essex remain. The original Norman castle was built in 1086 by Swayne, Sheriff of Essex from 1066 to 1086.

Rhuddlan Close   Robert Rhuddlan was cousin and lieutenant of Count Hugh of Chester. Rhuddlan Castle was the strongest of Edward I's castles in North Wales and the first built by the King's architect, James of St George. Its purpose was to guard the ancient ford of the river Clwyd and to command the route to the supply base at Chester. It was linked to the sea by a deep-water channel nearly three miles long. Now in ruins, it was a concentric castle with a square courtyard enclosed by high walls, towers at the north and south corners and huge gatehouses at the other corners. It was demolished by Cromwell during the Civil Wars.

Robertson Close   The Rev. Joseph Robertson was rector of St Mary's church in 1911.

Rochester Court   Rochester Castle, beside the river Medway in Kent, was rebuilt of stone in the late 11th century by Gundolf, Bishop of Rochester. He also rebuilt Rochester Cathedral and the Tower of London and founded St Bartholomew's Hospital at Chatham. The Archbishop of Canterbury was given custody of the castle in 1127, after which the keep was built. The castle was badly damaged by King John and again in 1264. It lay in ruins for 100 years but by 1400 had been restored by Edward III. Over the centuries it deteriorated again, and its ruins are now maintained by English Heritage.

Salden Court   Salden village near Mursley once had a manor and a large mansion, Salden House, which was built by Sir John Fortescue in 1556 when he was lord of the manor. (See Fortescue Drive.) The house was built round a courtyard and had a frontage of 175 feet with a series of stained-glass windows depicting the Fortescue coats of arms. In 1603, the newly crowned King James I and his Queen were staying at Salden House, and in the great hall there on 28 June James dubbed 22 knights. As Sir John Fortescue's fortunes waned, the house fell into ruin and was never rebuilt, save for a small part restored as Salden House farm which still stands today.

Sir John Fortescue of Salden, 16th-century lord of all the manors of Shenley.

Sandal Court   Sandal Castle, Wakefield in Yorkshire was the site of the battle of Wakefield in December 1460, in which Richard, Duke of York was killed. During the Civil Wars in the 1640s, Sandal was twice besieged by Parliamentary forces and then stripped of its defences. The 13th-century castle had a commanding position overlooking the river Calder and the remains of the motte and bailey can still be seen.

Selby Grove   Around 1732 Thomas James Selby came into possession of both Tattenhoe and Westbury manors. He was Sheriff of Buckinghamshire in 1739 and by this time held several other manors in north Buckinghamshire, including Lavendon, Great Horwood and Wavendon. He was a shy, scholarly but friendly man who enjoyed fox hunting. He never married but lived with a 'very handsome' woman at Wavendon. He died in 1772 having bequeathed his property to his close friend, William Lowndes, who thereafter added the name Selby to his own. Descendants of the Selby-Lowndes family live in the area to this day.

Sheepcote Close   Very possibly the name of a field.

Shenley Road   This is a length of the old Shenley road which ran from the Watling Sreet at Shenley Church End to Bletchley.

Shepherds Green   Shepherds Spinney was shown on John Knapp's plan and survey of the lands at Shenley in 1771, as was Shepherds Close, a large field which is now covered by the houses in this road. The field was in the tenancy of Henry Fosseye.

Shouler Close   The Shouler family were much involved in the life of the village in the first half of the 20th century. In 1873, Henry Shouler was school attendance officer. He was married to Minnie Franklin. In 1903,

Sir Humphrey Stafford. The Stafford family, earls and dukes of Buckingham, held several manors across the Milton Keynes area, including Tattenhoe, Shenley and Milton Keynes village. Below: Almshouses, Shenley Church End, founded by Thomas Stafford of Tattenhoe in 1615.

Mrs Henry Shouler was shopkeeper and sub-postmistress. Their daughter, Gertrude, took over as postmistress in 1918, following the death of her mother, and she was followed in 1948 by her nephew Maurice Goodway.

Stafford Grove   The Stafford family were earls and dukes of Buckingham from the mid-14th century until the title became extinct in about 1637. They were lords of the manor of Tattenhoe from 1478, and Thomas Stafford acquired Westbury Manor, Shenley in 1512, after which the two manors descended together for the next 400 years. During the Civil Wars Stafford was a Royalist, and under Cromwell in 1647 his lands at Shenley and Tattenhoe were seized for delinquency (failure of duty) and the case against him was not discharged until 1651, after payment of a large fine. By this time, the Staffords also owned the lands of Shenley Brook End and Milton Keynes. The Shenley lands remained in the family for another generation before passing to the Selbys.

Sutleye Court   The family of Walter de Sutleye were owners of a Shenley manor in about 1284.

Tattershall Close   Tattershall Castle, Lincolnshire is a vast, fortified tower which was built in about 1440 for Ralph Cromwell, Lord Treasurer of

England. It is an important example of an early brick building with the tower containing state apartments. It was rescued from demolition and restored by Lord Curzon between 1911 and 1914 and is now owned by the National Trust.

Tene Acres   Tene Acres is taken from the name of fields shown on John Knapp's 1771 plan and survey of the Shenley lands as Lower ten acres and Upper ten acres.

The Homestead   A Norman homestead existed at Shenley Church End. Such homesteads consisted of a manor house or farm usually built on a mound made by digging out a moat up to 30ft wide and 8ft deep. The manor house or farm, with barns, was built on top of the mound and was a defence against invaders, robbers or wolves. On John Knapp's plan and survey of the lordship of Shenley in 1771, there are several 'homesteads' identified as homes of the tenant farmers at that time.

Thirlby Lane   Thomas Thurlby was rector of St Mary's church, Shenley from 1386 to 1432.

Toot Hill Close   Named after Shenley Toot, a medieval motte and bailey castle built for the lord of the manor around the time of the Norman Conquest. In Old English *toot* meant a look-out hill. The earthworks of the medieval moat and fort here have been preserved.

Vache Lane   The Vache family were lords of the manor of Shenley from 1285. In the early 1400s Blanche, daughter of Sir Philip de la Vache, married young Richard Grey de Wilton, taking the manor of Shenley as her dowry. Walter de la Vache was rector of St Mary's church from 1309 to 1340.

Earthworks of the Toot, Shenley Church End.

Willets Rise   Joseph Willett was a local farmer living at Wood Pond Farm, Whaddon and listed in *Kelly's Directory for Berks, Bucks and Oxon 1903*. The Willetts were a long-established family in Shenley and Loughton during the 19th and 20th centuries.

SHENLEY LODGE

Shenley Lodge was the name of a house which stood north-east of Shenley Brook End and was shown on Ordnance Survey maps 141 and 142. Shenley Lodge estate was the site of a variety of individually designed, energy-efficient houses specially built for an Energy World exhibition in 1986.

THEME Scientists in the Field of Energy

Ackroyd Place   Herbert Ackroyd Stuart (1864-1927) worked as an engineer in his father's ironworks at Bletchley where he experimented with engines, petrol and paraffin heaters. One day, by accident, some hot slag fell on some oil, and a small explosion occurred, giving Ackroyd the idea of using an explosive flash to drive an engine. By 1890 he had devised an oil combustion engine which worked. Eight of these engines were made at Bletchley before he sold his patent to Hornsby & Sons at Grantham, where over 30,000 of them were built and sold under the name 'Hornsby-Ackroyd'.

Angstrom Close   Anders Jonas Angstrom (1814-74) was a Swedish physicist and astronomer. He was a founder of spectroscopy, his work on solar spectra leading to the discovery of hydrogen in the sun. He also studied geomagnetism. The angstrom, named after him, is a unit equal to one tenth of a nanometre, used for measuring wavelengths of light. He wrote on heat, magnetism and optics. His son, Knut, was also a physicist noted for his research on solar radiation.

Aston Close   Francis William Aston (1877-1945) was an English scientist noted for his work on isotopes. He invented the mass spectograph, with which he investigated the isotopic structures of elements and for which he won the Nobel Prize for Chemistry in 1922. The Aston Dark Space in electronic discharges is named after him.

Brayton Court   George Brayton (1830-92) was an American mechanical engineer who worked on developing internal combustion engines. He invented the continuous ignition combustion engine, which later formed the basis of the turbine engine. He manufactured and sold gas turbines, giving his name to the Brayton cycle, a power cycle which operates the gas turbine. A Brayton engine has a compressor, a combustion chamber (burner) and a turbine, and is also used in jet engines.

Bunsen Place   Robert Wilhelm Bunsen (1811-99) was a German chemist and physicist. He became Professor of Chemistry at Heidelberg in 1852. With Gustav Kirchhoff he discovered spectrum analysis, which made possible the discovery of new elements. He invented the Bunsen burner, the grease-spot photometer, a galvanic battery, an ice calorimeter and, with the English scientist Sir Henry Roscoe, the actinometer.

Cadman Square   This probably refers to Mr Walter Cadman, who was lord of the manor of Loughton during the 19th century. Thomas Cademan (1590-1650) was a British research chemist in the field of distillation, a method of purifying or separating the components of a liquid by boiling, evaporating the liquid and condensing the vapour. Today distillation is used in petrol refineries to separate hydrocarbons, in the purification of sea water and, as it probably was in Cademan's day, the manufacture of alcoholic spirits.

Carnot Close   Nicolas Leonard Sadi Carnot (1796-1832) was a French scientist and soldier. He was the founder of the science of thermodynamics. His investigations into the efficiency of steam engines led him to the conclusion that no engine can be more efficient than a reversible engine working between the same temperatures, or the Carnot Cycle and Carnot's Theorem. In the French army, Carnot became a captain of engineers. He died from cholera.

Caroline Haslett Combined School   The school, which opened in 1992, was named after Dame Caroline Haslett (1895-1957). She was a lifelong champion of women's potential in the field of engineering and electrical science and, at a time when electricity was in its infancy, had the foresight to see how electricity in the home could make lives easier for women. In 1932 she became the first woman accepted as a companion member of the Institute of Electrical Engineers, and the same year was elected chairwoman of the Home Safety Committee. Caroline Haslett was made a Dame in 1947.

Clegg Square   Samuel Clegg (1781-1861) was a British gas engineer. He designed the gas-holder, which at first people feared was dangerous. To allay such fears, and knowing that gas will not explode unless mixed with the right proportion of air, he took a pick and punctured a hole in the side of a gas-holder, then lit the escaping gas. In 1817 he installed a gas works at the Royal Mint and developed an efficient gas meter. He also designed a lime purification process, the hydraulic main, D-shaped horizontal retorts and several other features of 19th-century gas works practice, some of which survived into the 1970s. Clegg equipped many mills and factories with gas lighting. Coal gas was generated on the premises; there was no gas grid at that time.

Cockerel Grove   Sir Christopher Cockerel (1910-99) was an English radio-engineer who pioneered the hovercraft. During the Second World War he worked in radar and afterwards concentrated on hydrodynamics. In 1955 he filed a patent for an air-cushion vehicle and in 1959 the hovercraft was launched. His first experiment to this end was of the 'don't try this at home' variety. He put a tin of cat food inside a coffee tin attached to a vacuum cleaner with the airflow reversed which was poised above a set of kitchen scales. Cockerel was knighted in 1969, but made little money from the invention and lived his retirement on his state pension.

Crowther Court   Phineas Crowther, of Newcastle-upon-Tyne, patented an improved type of vertical engine in 1800. It had no beam and was quickly and widely used as a colliery winding engine. Also, Edward Crowther (1897-1979) was a British gas engineer.

Darby Close   Abraham Darby (1678-1717) achieved the first successful smelting of iron with coke. He started out as an apprentice in the brewing industry, but then set up a brass and iron foundry in Bristol. Next he took a lease on an abandoned furnace at Coalbrookdale, Shropshire, where he developed his smelting process. His innovation was slow to be taken up, but by the 1770s coke furnaces had replaced charcoal furnaces. By the time he died, Abraham Darby owned three iron foundries in Coalbrookdale.

Edison Square   Thomas Alva Edison (1847-1931) was an American inventor. When he was 12 years old, he saved the life of a stationmaster's son and, as a reward, was taught how to operate the telegraph. He worked for several years as a telegraph operator before setting up his own workshop in which to invent. The results include the printing-telegraph, the carbon telephone transmitter, the microphone, the gramophone and, most famously, the electric light bulb. By 1881 Edison had built a generating station and supplied electricity to over 80 customers. In all he has 1,300 inventions to his name. He discovered thermionic emission and was involved in the development of motion pictures.

Faraday Drive   Michael Faraday (1791-1867) was a chemist and physicist whose greatest work was in the field of electricity and magnetism. In 1841 he discovered the induction of electric currents, which led to the invention of the electric motor. This opened the way to the discovery of wireless waves, X-rays, television and atomic physics. Faraday started as a laboratory assistant to Sir Humphrey Davy and went on to succeed Davy as Director of the Royal Institution Laboratory in 1825.

Grantham Court   Sir Isaac Newton (1642-1727) was born at Woolsthorpe Manor near Grantham, Lincolnshire and went to the Free Grammar School in Grantham. Much of his early scientific work was carried out at home here. Regarded as England's greatest scientist and mathematician, Newton is most famous for his discovery of the law of gravitation, although his other work included the study of fluxions, the study of the nature of light and the construction of telescopes. (It was at Grantham that 30,000 of Ackroyd's combustion engines were produced after he had sold his patent to Hornsby & Sons. See Ackroyd Place.)

Hansen Croft   Gerhard A. Hansen (1841-1912) was a Norwegian bacteriologist who, in 1874, discovered the bacterium *Mycobacterium leprae*, which causes leprosy (also known as Hansen's disease).

Hauksbee Gardens   Francis Hauksbee was a 17th-century English physicist who studied electricity and invented the first glass electrical machine. He also made improvements to the air pump. He became a Fellow of the Royal Society in 1705 and died in about 1713. Francis Hauksbee the younger (1687-1763), believed to be his son, also worked in the electrical field and was appointed clerk and housekeeper to the Royal Society in 1723.

Hollister Chase   Charles Davis Hollister (1936-99) was an American marine geologist, oceanographer and sedimentologist. His explorations of the deep-sea floor led him to study the strong currents there and the effect on the movement and rifting of sediment. He extracted a 100 ft core sample, which held a 65 million-year-long history of the ocean bed and prompted the development of a giant piston coring system.

Joules Court   A joule is a unit of energy named after the physicist James Prescott Joule (1818-89). He was famous for his experiments which showed that heat is a form of energy and determined the amount of mechanical and, later, electrical energy needed to propagate heat energy. His experiments became the basis for the Theory of the Conservation of Energy. Joule was elected Fellow of the Royal Society in 1850.

Kaplan Close   Viktor Kaplan (1876-1937) designed the Kaplan turbine used in the generation of hydro-electricity. The Kaplan is a reaction turbine, a feathering-propeller type which looks like a ship's screw. The angle of the blades can be altered to suit the material flowing through it.

Kindermann Court   It has been suggested that a Ferdinand Kindermann was involved in the invention of the double piston engine, but no information has been found to support this. A Ferdinand Kindermann (1740-1801) was a Bohemian priest who founded an elementary school where agriculture and natural science were taught alongside the three Rs, music and religion. He earned the title 'father of industrial education'.

Krypton Close   Krypton is an inert, gaseous element occurring in trace amounts in air and used in fluorescent lights and lasers. Symbol Kr, atomic no. 36, atomic weight 83.80.

Langmuir Court   Irving Langmuir (1881-1957) was an American chemist who won the Nobel Prize in 1932 for his work on surface chemistry. He was associated with the General Electric Company from 1909 to 1950 and from 1932 was a director of their research laboratory. His many inventions include the gas-filled tungsten lamp and atomic hydrogen welding.

Laser Close   A laser is a device for converting light of mixed frequencies into an intense, narrow, monochromatic beam. The term is also used for any similar device producing a beam of electromagnetic radiation, such as infra-red or microwave radiation.

Lawson Place   H.J. Lawson was the first man to build a chain-driven bicycle. It was known as Harry Lawson's bicyclette. Bicycle manufacture was the principal industry in Coventry until the late 1890s when there was a slump in demand. With an entrepreneurial eye, Harry Lawson switched his interest to automobiles, formed a business syndicate and opened the first commercial car factory in Britain, thus becoming the founder of the Coventry car industry. He also designed the first Humber cars produced in the early 20th century.

Livesey Hill   George Livesey (1834-1908) was a British gas engineer who developed the storage gasometer. He also implemented the principle of worker-shareholders and financed the founding of Livesey library in the Old Kent Road, London.

Marconi Croft   Guglielmo Marconi (1874-1937) was an Italian electrical engineer who invented radio communication. After the discovery of radio waves, Marconi designed and built an instrument that would convert them into electrical signals, which he then transmitted over ever-increasing distances. In 1901 one of his signals was picked up across the Atlantic Ocean. He was awarded a Nobel Prize for Physics in 1909.

Maudsley Close   Henry Maudslay (1771-1831) was a British engineer who invented the metal lathe. He established his own machine-tools business and his other inventions include the slide-rule, a method of desalinating sea water and the precision screw-cutting lathe in 1810. This revolutionised engineering by turning out nuts and bolts with perfect threads. Maudslay also designed marine engines and invented the variable-pitch propeller.

Maybach Court   Wilhelm Maybach was a German engineer who invented the carburettor in 1856. He worked with Gottlieb Daimler and produced an early petrol-powered motor car featuring his carburettor. He also worked on motor bikes with Daimler.

Mayer Gardens   Julius Robert von Mayer (1814-78) was a German physicist. He was the first to calculate the mechanical equivalent of heat and propose a form of the law of conservation of energy. But Mayer's work was virtually unrecognised because credit for the first achievement was given to Joule. As a result of the disputes over priority, Mayer's mental health suffered.

Menzies Court   Michael Menzies was a Scottish inventor who, in 1732, designed a simple tool in which flails were secured to a shaft. The whole was driven by a water wheel, making the earliest form of threshing machine.

Murrey Close   Matthew Murray (1765-1826) was a British mechanical engineer. He developed a smaller, lighter, more efficient and easily assembled steam engine after Watt's patent expired in 1800. Murray's engine enabled steam power to be used in locomotives and ships, whereas before only stationary work could be done.

Northcroft   Possibly named after a field, North Close, shown on a plan and survey of Shenley drawn up for the landowner John Knapp in 1771.

Osier Lane   This is a section of an existing Osier Lane. Marked on the Milton Keynes City map, fourth edition (1984), the old lane branched off the old Whaddon to Bletchley road to join Watling Street at a point opposite Knowlhill. An osier is another name for a willow tree whose twigs are used in basket-making.

Parsons Crescent   Sir Charles Algernon Parsons (1854-1931) was a British engineer who invented the steam turbine in 1884. He used the turbine to power his ship *Turbania* in 1897 and reached a record-breaking speed of 35 knots. He was the fourth son of the 3rd Earl of Rosse and director of a large engineering works in Newcastle-upon-Tyne, and was knighted in 1911.

Paxton Crescent   Sir Joseph Paxton (1801-65) was born in the village of Milton Bryan, near Woburn. He was a gardener and architect and, while working for the Duke of Devonshire, he remodelled the gardens at Chatsworth and managed the estate. He experimented with new techniques of construction using iron and glass in building greenhouses at Chatsworth, before he designed and built the Crystal Palace in Hyde Park to house the Great Exhibition 1851. Paxton also designed country houses such as Mentmore Towers near Wing, Buckinghamshire.

Pelton Court   Lester Allen Pelton (1829-1918) was an American engineer who patented the Pelton wheel in 1889. This is a hydraulic turbine used in the generation of hydro-electricity. The wheel consists of a ring of buckets, or bucket-shaped cups, arranged around the periphery. It is known as an impulse turbine because it is only the impulse of the water that makes the wheel turn.

Redwood Gate   This name is possibly a derivation of Redocks Hill, which was a 14-acre woodland existing in Shenley during the 16th century.

Runford Court   Benjamin Thompson, Count Rumford (1753-1814) was an American scientist who spied for the British during the American Revolution and was forced to flee to England. He carried out scientific research into ballistics and the theory of heat. Suspected of spying for the French, he left England for Paris and then Bavaria, where he worked for the Elector, who made him a count of the Holy Roman Empire in 1791. He chose the title Rumford after his home town in America. Returning to England in 1795, he helped to demolish the caloric theory and founded the Royal Institution.

Rutherford Gate   Ernest, 1st Baron Rutherford of Nelson (1871-1937) , a New Zealander by birth, was the greatest experimental physicist of all time. He split the atom with apparatus costing only a few pounds and opened up a whole new science – that of nuclear physics. He became Cavendish Professor of Physics at Cambridge in 1919 and dominated nuclear research there for a generation.

Silicon Court   Silicon is the second most abundant element in the earth's crust after oxygen. It was discovered in 1824. Pure silicon is of great importance in the electronics industry as a semi-conductor. The silicon chip is a tiny wafer of silicon processed to form a type of integrated circuit or component such as a transistor.

Symington Court   William Symington (1763-1831) was a Scottish engineer and inventor. In 1787 he patented an engine for road locomotion and then a similar engine on a 25ft long boat. In 1802 he completed building of the *Charlotte Dundas,* the first workable steamboat ever built. Symington intended it for use as a tug, but a few people with a vested interest scuppered his plans, saying that the wash created by the boat would damage the sides of the Forth and Clyde canal. He died in poverty in London.

Trevithick Lane   Richard Trevithick (1771-1833) was a Cornish engineer and inventor. While working in a Cornish mine he developed a water-pressure engine, and then turned his attention to steam power. He was the first man to have a steam locomotive tried out on a railway. His engine pulled five wagons carrying 10 tonnes of iron and 70 men for nearly nine miles at a speed of about five miles an hour. Nobody took his invention very seriously so he went to South America to help the revolutionaries in their fight for independence from Spain. When he came home no one remembered him or his inventions, although his engines were used in the Peruvian mines.

Upton Grove   Francis Robbins Upton (1852-1921) was an American electrical engineer who worked with Edison on the development of the incandescent lamp and the power-timer electricity meter. Upton was the first student to earn by examination a Master of Science degree from Princeton University, in 1877. Edison was an intuitive genius without a scientific education and he relied on Upton to interpret his ideas and translate them into mathematical equations. Upton's house in New Jersey was the first house in the world to be lit by electric light, after their invention of the light bulb, and the first classroom to be so lit was that of Upton's mentor at Princeton, Professor Cyrus Fogg Brackett.

Volta Rise   Alessandro, Count Volta (1745-1827) was an Italian physicist. He was Professor of Natural Philosophy at Pavia from 1774-1804. He developed the theory of current electricity, discovered the electric decomposition of water, invented an electric battery, the electrophorus and an electroscope and also made investigations into heat and gases. His name is given to the unit of electric pressure, the volt.

Winstanley Lane   Henry Winstanley (1644-1703) was an English architect and engraver. He built the first Eddystone lighthouse and lost his life there when it was swept away in a severe storm on 2 November 1703. Incidentally, the Rev. George Winstanley was rector of St Mary's church, Shenley between 1605 and 1629.

SHENLEY WOOD

Shenley Wood is shown on John Knapp's 1771 Plan and Survey of Shenley lands.

THEME **Woodland Associations**

Chalkdell Drive   A chalk dell is a scooped-out hollow in chalky ground.

Foxcovert Road   Shenley Wood was once known as Foxcovert, after it was planted up specially to provide cover for foxhunting by the Whaddon Chase, Grafton and Oakley Hunts. In 1903, the wood was put up for sale by its owner, Stanley Ormond. A covert is a thicket, or spinney, where foxes might hide. A fox breaks cover when flushed out by hounds, or runs to cover to hide from pursuit.

Merlewood Drive Merle is another name for the blackbird, so Merlewood means blackbird wood.

Wildacre Road   An acre of wild, uncultivated land.

TATTENHOE

Tattenhoe is the name of the original village, Norman manor and parish. The site of the manor is shown on Ordnance Survey map 17. The site of the old medieval village is preserved in a corner of the Tattenhoe District Park and is shown on the official Milton Keynes map. The name derives from the Anglo-Saxon Tata's-hoh, meaning 'Tata's spur of land'.

THEME **Headlands and Points around the Heritage Coasts of Britain**

Because Tattenhoe Manor anciently belonged to the Martell family, who founded the nearby Priory of Snelshall, the Milton Keynes Development Corporation originally chose Medieval Monasteries as the theme for Tattenhoe. However, the later administration decided to transfer the Monasteries theme to Monkston and adapt Monkston's original theme of Bird and Wildlife Sanctuaries for Tattenhoe. Hence the theme here is Headlands and Points around the Heritage Coasts of Britain, many of which have bird or wildlife sanctuaries and are Sites of Special Scientific Interest, as is Tattenhoe's Howe Park Wood.

Balcary Grove   Balcary Point at the tip of Auchencairn Bay on the coast of Dumfries and Galloway, Scotland is a headland on the Solway Firth.

Gentle grassland slopes, scattered with wild violets, primroses and orchids in spring, lead to dramatic and dangerous cliff-tops, alive with the clamour of nesting kittiwakes, fulmers, herring gulls, guillemots, razorbills and cormorants and colours of the wild flowers clinging to the cliff-face. The RSPB Mersehead Nature Reserve is renowned for its waterfowl, especially wintering barnacle geese.

Blakeney Court Blakeney village and Blakeney Point are on the North Norfolk Heritage Coast. The village was a commercial port until the beginning of the 20th century, but the estuary has since silted up to a narrow channel and is only navigable by small sailing craft. Wide marshes spread out to the Point, which is reached by a three-and-a-half-mile long sand and shingle spit. A wildfowl breeding ground, noted for colonies of terns and rare migrant birds, it has been a National Trust Nature Reserve since 1912. Common and grey seals can also be seen and trips by boat are organised.

Blyth Court Blyth has been a port since the 12th century, growing to become a major outlet for coal from Northumberland's mines, the last of which closed in the 1980s. It is now used for landing aluminium ore for a smelting works up the coast at Lynemouth and as a supply base for the North Sea oil and gas fields. Blyth's most striking features today are its strong wooden pier, which matches anything the Romans might have built, and its regimental line of nine windmills standing defensively across the harbour mouth as they generate electricity for the National Grid. The High Light lighthouse, built in 1788 beside the river, stands behind a residential street since being marooned after land was reclaimed for a new harbour in the 1880s.

Carnweather Court Carnweather Point lies off Port Quin, on the north Cornish coast. The waters here have strong currents and an eddy of tremendous proportions. The flow reverses some 90 minutes before high tide, creating such a powerful current that shoals of fish will suddenly turn and swim close in to the Point.

Channory Close Channory, Chanoney or Chanonry Point (according to which map you read) is on the Moray Firth in Scotland, north-east of Inverness on the peninsula known as the Black Isle because it rarely gets any winter snow. This is regarded as one of the best places in Britain from which to watch the antics of bottle-nosed dolphins and dolphin 'safaris' can be arranged. At Fortrose there are beaches and the vaulted crypt of a ruined 13th-century cathedral.

Coverack Place Coverack is a fishing village on the south Cornish coast and is built on both sides of a spur of rock which juts out into the sea. It has a disused lighthouse, a small harbour built of Serpentine stone and an old lifeboat house with slipway which are all reminders of Coverack's maritime history, one of smuggling and ships wrecked on the Manacles, jagged rocks submerged beneath the waves.

Dodman Green   Dodman Point near Coverack, south Cornwall rises nearly 400 feet above sea level and is topped by a giant cross, erected in 1896 to commemorate a Royal Navy tragedy at sea. On the South West Coast Path, Dodman Point is notorious for its ship wrecks. There is also an extensive Iron-Age fort with the earthworks of a defensive baulk.

Dungeness Court   Dungeness is one of the largest stretches of shingle in the world and is designated a National Nature Reserve, Special Protection Area and Special Area of Conservation. Protruding into the Strait of Dover off Walland and Romney marshes, Dungeness has a unique variety of wildlife, including very rare moths, beetles and spiders, and more than 600 varieties of plant, all of which are regarded as extremely fragile because of the area's popularity with visitors. The landscape, of shingle ridges which have built up over 5,000 years, is also scientifically important. Dungeness Bird Observatory promotes, records and shares information on the area. Dungeness Old Lighthouse may be visited.

Dunnet Close   Dunnet Head is Scotland's most northerly point, with magnificent views across the Pentland Firth. Although the lighthouse, built in 1832, stands 300 feet above the sea, windows have been smashed by stones thrown up by the angry waters. Military bunkers remain from Dunnet Head's involvement in the defence of the naval base at Scapa Flow during the Second World War.

Durlston   Durlston Country Park with Durlston Head, on the southern tip of the Isle of Purbeck, is a 280-acre World Heritage Site on the Dorset Heritage Coast. With limestone cliffs, downland, woodland, fields and hedgerows, it is a haven teeming with wildlife. There are birds, plants, insects and animals as well as extraordinary geology and cliff formations. The remains of a Napoleonic telegraph station and Anvil Point lighthouse are also of interest.

East Chapel   The field names of Chapel Ground, Chapel Meadow and Chapel Thrift appear in a

Buried in the trees, the tiny St Giles church, Tattenhoe, is of Norman date, but completed in the mid-16th century.

Survey and List of Places of Archaeological Interest in the Tattenhoe area. The name possibly refers to a 13th-century chapel at Tattenhoe, on the site of which the present St Giles' church was built in 1540 using the stones of the nearby ruin of Snelshall Priory.

Eastoke Place   Eastoke Point off the Eastoke Peninsula is at the Hayling Island entrance to Chichester Harbour, Sussex. The peninsula has been gradually developed as a residential area since the 1920s, but now is fighting a battle against flooding, a shingle beach on the southern shore being the only defence against the onslaught of high tides and stormy seas causing coastal erosion. Parts of the peninsula are still unspoilt and there is a nature reserve.

Godrevy Grove   On the Godrevy-Portreath Heritage Coast to the north of St Ives Bay, this temperamental area can change from a place of restful calm on a summer's day to one of angry rage when a storm flares up. Godrevy Point juts out into a sea of unpredictable currents and, although there is a small beach, it can be dangerous for swimmers. The lighthouse on the tiny offshore island of Godrevy was once home to a keeper, but now automatically warns ships away from this coastline, which is protected by the National Trust.

Goodwick Grove   Goodwick, on the Pembrokeshire coast near Fishguard, has an underwater Ocean Laboratory where sea creatures from millions of years ago are brought to life, and visitors can explore the deep by submarine. The ferry sails from Goodwick to Rosslare in Ireland.

Great Ormes   Great Ormes Head, a bold peninsula thrusting out into Conwy Bay off the North Wales coast, is a designated Site of Special Scientific Interest, Special Area of Conservation and a Heritage Coast. Mostly covered by the Great Ormes Country Park and Nature Reserve, it contains valuable geology, archaeology and wildlife, including endangered species such as the Grayling butterfly and unusual spiders as well as seabirds and little owls. Bronze-Age copper mines with tunnels dug 4,000 years ago and leading to a cavern can be explored and a multiplying herd of Kashmiri goats roams with feral goats on the headland. The lighthouse, built in 1862, is a fortress-like building of limestone and pitched pine, which flashed its warning light for the last time in 1985 when its optic was removed. It is now a hotel complex.

Gunver Lane   Gunver Head is a headland off Trevone Bay, on the north Cornwall coast.

Hartland Avenue   The Hartland area of the North Devon Heritage Coast juts out from Bideford Bay, where the Bristol Channel meets the wild Atlantic Ocean, and includes Hartland Point, Hartland village and Hartland Abbey. The treacherous coastline is very rugged and the lighthouse, built in 1873, stands on an outcrop of rock beneath a 350ft cliff. The light has a range of 26 miles and has been automatic since 1982. The wreck of *The Johanna*, which hit the rocks in 1982, can still be seen. In a field on the edge of the village is Hartland Magnetic Observatory, which moved from Greenwich Observatory in 1957 because electrification of the railways made accurate geomagnetic measurements impossible. The observatory at Hartland was specifically built for magnetic work.

Hengistbury Lane   Hengistbury Head, a 120ft-high headland at the tip of Poole Bay on the Dorset coast, forms a natural breakwater protecting Christchurch and its harbour from the inrush of the sea. Concerns over its erosion have dogged the Head for hundreds of years, particularly in the 19th century when iron ore was being mined in the area, and again in 1930 when much of it crumbled into the sea. With Christchurch harbour, Hengistbury Head is now a designated Site of Special Scientific Interest and, because it is feared that it is doomed eventually to be claimed by the sea, access to it is severely restricted.

Highveer Croft   Above the Heddon Valley in north Devon, on the west Exmoor coast, Highveer Point rises 100 feet above the coastal path. It is a unique National Trust property of towering cliffs, wooded combes and extensive coastal heather moorland, where buzzards, ravens, guillemots and fulmers may be seen.

Holborn Crescent   Holborn Head runs out off the west side of Thurso Bay, Caithness in Scotland, from where there are views to Dunnet Head and across the Pentland Firth. Holborn Head lighthouse is at Scrabster harbour.

Holyhead Crescent   Holyhead, the main town on Holy Island, Anglesey is where the boats sail to and from Ireland and the A5 falls into the Irish Sea. It is a bird-watchers' paradise. There is an RSPB sanctuary at South Stack where seabirds nest on rocky ledges and seals inhabit the caves; there are colonies of puffins and guillemots and a lighthouse and lifeboat station. The whole of Anglesey is a designated Area of Outstanding Natural Beauty.

Howe Park Wood   Once known as Hoo Park Wood, this ancient woodland in Tattenhoe is a designated Site of Special Scientific Interest which sets the theme chosen for this estate. It is particularly noted for the colonies of dragonflies which have been attracted to the three ponds

A path through Howe Park Wood.

excavated in 1990 on the north-west flank of the wood. Among the varieties that can be seen are the emperor dragonfly, the broad-bodied chaser, black-tailed skimmer and the emerald damselfly.

Howe Rock Place   Howe Rock lies in the Bristol Channel off Burnham-on-Sea.

Langerstone Lane   Langerstone Point is a rugged headland off the south Devon coast near Salcombe.

Langney Green   Langney Point, east of Eastbourne and jutting out into Pevensey Bay, has a Martello tower, number 66. Martello towers are circular forts which were built in the early 19th century for coastal defence during the Napoleonic Wars. There were 74 in all along the south coast between Seaford and Folkestone. Tower 66 Langney Point was built at the same time as Tower 67 to increase the firepower of the six-gun battery known as East Langney Fort, or Langney Redoubt, which had been built in 1795. In later wars, the towers were used as look-out posts. Langney Point has a Second World War watchtower roof and was used by coastguards until 1989, but now, despite being classified as an ancient monument, it is a derelict building.

Linney Court   Linney Head is a columnar basalt rock formation which extends for about six miles east along the coast to St Govan's Head. A spectacular stretch of the Pembrokeshire Coast National Park with many caves and an abundance of bird life, the rocks here have claimed many storm-stricken ships.

Logan Rock   A monumental lump of granite, known as the Logan Rock, lies on a headland south of Treen and east of Porthcurno on the Lands End peninsula. A 'logan' rock is a rocking stone which 'logs' or rocks at the slightest touch. *Log* is a dialect word meaning rock. The one at Treen is estimated to weigh somewhere between 65 and 80 tons and the story goes that, in 1824, a Naval Lieutenant Goldsmith, with a group of sailors, for some obscure reason pushed it over the cliff. The locals were so outraged that Lt Goldsmith was ordered to reinstate the rock at his own expense.

Longpeak Close   Lower Longbeak and Higher Longbeak are points along the north Cornwall coastal path in the Widemouth Bay, Bude area.

Lowland Road   Lowland Point is on the south Cornwall coastal path, on National Trust land at the north-east tip of Coverack Bay. The path here has a low cliff edge and is a one-hour walk from Coverack village.

Mavoncliff Drive   This is possibly Mayon Cliff, on the south Cornwall coastal path near Sennen.

Merthen Grove   Merthen Point and ancient oak woodland is at the mouth of the Helford river, south Cornwall. A designated Site of Special Scientific Interest and a Special Area of Conservation, it contains ferns, mosses and abundant wildlife.

Nash Croft   This may have been the name of a field. In an undated Particular of Lands at Loughton and Nether Shenley, Nash fields are listed as occupied by John Stevens. However, Nash Point on the Glamorgan Heritage Coast of Wales was formed after an upheaval of the tropical sea bed raised the land to a height of 492 feet above sea level. On the shore, the rocks formed into slabs like causeways, with many small rock pools at low tide. There are two lighthouses, one without its light, the other still working, as is its very loud fog horn.

Oldcastle Croft   Oldcastle Point lies off the South Pembrokeshire Heritage Coast, in the bay east of the village of Manorbier. The name probably refers to the ruins of the moated Norman castle at Manorbier where, in about 1146, was born Giraldus Cambrensis, a noted Welsh scholar and topographer.

Oxwich Lane   Oxwich Point is on the Gower Heritage Coast of Wales and Oxwich National Nature Reserve occupies most of Oxwich Bay. In the dunes, marshes and woodlands there are many species of birds and insects and more than 600 flower varieties have been discovered.

Penhale Close   South of Newquay, Penhale Point is at the southern tip of Holywell Bay. Much of the land around the point is taken by the MOD Penhale Camp and Training Area, which is used by all three services, and the coastal path takes a detour around the perimeter fence. The Penhale sand dunes are among the highest in England and are a designated Site of Special Scientific Interest.

Penlee Rise   Penlee Point is on the tip of Cawsand Bay at the mouth of Plymouth Sound on the Rame Head Heritage Coast. Penlee Battery Nature Reserve covers an area of coastal grassland, scrub and woodland on the site of a disused battery which was a coastal fortification operating in the 1920s. There are steps, which were used for unloading heavy guns from barges when Penlee was being armed, and a slope for horse traffic. For many people, the name Penlee recalls the tragedy of the Penlee lifeboat, which is stationed many miles down the coast at Newlyn harbour. In December 1981 the *Solomon Browne* was called out in hurricane force winds to rescue the crew of the coaster *Union Star*. The lifeboat was tossed and smashed against the deck of the coaster, then disappeared beneath the water. All eight lifeboatmen were drowned, along with all crew members of the *Union Star*.

Plymouth Grove   Historically Plymouth, on the south Devon coast, is England's most famous naval port. Numerous ships and sailors were launched from here to fight in the Hundred Years War against France; from Plymouth Hoe, while playing bowls, Sir Francis Drake espied the Spanish Armada on its way to invade us; from here in 1620 the Pilgrim Fathers sailed away on the *Mayflower* to the New World; in 1772 James Cook set out to circumnavigate the globe, and in 1966 Sir Francis Chichester sailed from Plymouth to do the same thing, but single-handed on his yacht, *Gypsy*

Moth. The Germans tried to obliterate Plymouth in the Second World War, but it rose again and is still housing frigates and nuclear submarines in the Royal Naval Dockyards. All this history is exhibited for today's visitors in The Dome on Plymouth Hoe, where the famous landmark of Smeaton's Tower also stands. Originally built on the Eddystone rocks, it was dismantled stone-by-stone and rebuilt on the Hoe. The National Marine Aquarium has the deepest tank in Europe, housing sharks, tropical fish, turtles and sea-horses. There are historic houses to visit, a leisure park and boat trips to take and, if that's all too much, there's the Gin Distillery, still making original Plymouth gin.

Porthcawl Green   At the western tip of the Heritage Coast, Porthcawl is a traditional seaside holiday place near Bridgend. Porthcawl Point juts out into the sea.

Porthmellin Close   Porthmellin Head is one of a series of headlands near St Anthony's-in-Roseland, along a dramatic, lonely stretch of Cornish coastline of rocky and mostly unreachable coves tucked beneath shoulders of wild and empty moorland.

Portishead Drive   Portishead, just south of Avonmouth in the mouth of the river Severn, became commercialised in the mid-19th century when a power station and a deep-water dock were built for large ships importing and exporting iron and steel and other raw materials from round the world. The power station was closed in 1980 and the dock became redundant. It is now being developed into a marina for yachts and leisure craft. Portishead (or Battery) Point has been a strategic site since the 16th century.

Roscolyn Drive   Rhoscolyn, North Wales, is a rocky headland at the southern tip of Holy Island, which is linked to Anglesey by a causeway. There is a sheltered cove with a large, sloping beach backed by sand dunes and edged with rock pools.

Rosemullion Avenue   Rosemullion Head lies to the north of Helford Passage, on the south Cornish coast. It is an area of National Trust land with the three gardens of Trebah, Curwinian and Glendurgen. The rocky shores support a wide range of plant and animal life, including the rare Giant Goby.

St Anthony's Place   St Anthony's-in-Roseland, on the Roseland peninsula, south Cornwall is on the tip of the Carrick Roads estuary. The lighthouse, once a coal beacon which burned for centuries until the present lighthouse was built in 1834, warns ships off the dreaded Manacles rocks, which have claimed many victims. St Anthony Head was a strategic battery, protecting Falmouth and the Carrick Roads during both world wars, when guns were stationed here and army training took place. The headland is now National Trust land.

St Govans Close   St Govan's Head on the Pembrokeshire coast, out on the cliffs of the Pembrokeshire National Park, is within a Site of Special Scientific Interest, a Special Protection Area and candidate Special Area of Conservation, supporting as it does a number of pairs of breeding choughs. There are also cliff-ledge nest sites of guillemots, razorbills and peregrine falcons. At the bottom of the cliffs is a 12th-century chapel with a 'healing' well, which has been a place of pilgrimage since at least the sixth century.

St Ives Crescent On the Penwith Heritage Coast, Cornwall, St Ives Head protrudes into the sea above the little town of St Ives, with its colourful jumble of cottages in narrow, twisting streets. Founded around a small chapel built in the sixth century by St Ia, St Ives was once a fishing port and has been an artists' centre and workshop since James Whistler and William Sickert set the artistic fashion here in the 19th century.

St Thomas Court St Thomas Head is on the south Cornwall coast.

Sharkham Court Sharkham Point is near Brixham on the South Devon Heritage Coast. With Berry Head, it is a designated Site of Special Scientific Interest for its wildlife and geological distinction. A Special Area of Conservation is proposed for it under EC Habitats Directive. Sharkham Point Iron Mine Country Park at Berry Head is a nature reserve.

Sheerness Court Sheerness, on the Isle of Sheppey at the mouth of the river Medway in the Thames estuary, was a Royal Naval dockyard, established in the 17th century by Samuel Pepys, an Admiralty official as well as a Diarist. After 1960 it became a commercial port. A three-mile stretch of the coast, where cliffs rise steeply from the beach, is a Conservation Coast and fossils are found here. Emley Marshes RSPB Nature Reserve provides hides where many resident and migrant sea birds can be watched, including the avocet, and English Nature's Swale National Nature Reserve affords sightings not only of sea birds but also buntings, owls and many more.

Steeple Close Steeple Point rises some 30 feet above sea level on the coastal path near Bude, north Cornwall.

Stolford Rise Stolford, near Hinckley Point on the west Somerset coast of Bridgwater Bay, has a pebble beach and a bird sanctuary. Much of the land here is mud flats and Stolford Flats have been monitored since 1980 by Piscen Conservation for its fish and crustacean population. About 80 species of fish and 25 species of macro-crustacea have been recorded. There is a small stake-net fishery and the area is popular with anglers and birdwatchers.

Sunderland Court Sunderland Point off the Lancashire coast, where the river Lune flows into the Irish Sea, is a headland almost entirely surrounded by water. Reached across the salt marshes from the village of Overton, the Point was a port in the 18th century for ships bound for the West Indies and was the landing place for the first ever cargo of cotton imported into England to be manufactured in Lancashire's cotton mills.

Thorpness Croft   The Haven, Thorpness, a seemingly barren stretch of the Suffolk coast, is in fact a Site of Special Scientific Interest with a remarkable variety of plants surviving the harsh conditions of salty winds, shingle, dunes, scrubland and grassland. Insects such as the great green bush cricket also thrive, as do birds, including the marsh harrier and migrants in transit. The Haven is in the care of the Suffolk Wildlife Trust on behalf of the RSPB, who also own the nearby North Warren Nature Reserve. Thorpness post windmill was moved from Sizewell in the 1920s and converted to pump water to the village from the 'House in the Clouds', an extraordinary water tower which was disguised to look like a tall house, but appears as though it might have been designed by Professor Caractacus Potts.

Walney Place   Walney Island, off Barrow-in-Furness in Morecambe Bay, is home to two nature reserves. The 350 acres of North Walney reserve includes sand dunes, saltmarsh, scrub, heath and shingle, is a nationally important wildlife site and is of archaeological and geological interest. South Walney reserve has the largest colony of herring and lesser black-backed gulls in Europe, with around 30,000 breeding pairs, and one of the largest eider duck colonies in England. Waterfowl and waders over-winter here and many migrant birds visit in spring and autumn. Enriched by gull droppings, both reserves support an abundance of plant and insect life.

Winfold Lane Linking Tattenhoe with Emerson Valley, this refers to Winfold Fell in the Trough of Bowland, Lancashire.

WESTCROFT

An early medieval name, Westcroft is mentioned in the Snelshall Cartulary, a document of c.1250. Westcroft was in the vicinity of Tattenhoe green

THEME Historic Gardens

Abbotsbury   The sub-tropical gardens at Abbotsbury in Dorset were established in 1765 by the first Countess of Ilchester. Today it is a 20-acre garden containing rare and exotic plants, many of which were discovered and brought to Britain by the descendants of the countess.

Alton Gate   The extensive gardens at Alton Towers, Staffordshire were first opened to the public in 1860. Garden designers Thomas Allason and Robert Abrahams developed them into the lavish extravaganza they are today. Miles of walking can be avoided by viewing the gardens from the Sky Ride.

Babylon Grove   The Hanging Gardens of Babylon are one of the Seven Wonders of the World. According to fable, they were constructed in the sixth century BC by King Nebuchadnezzar for one of his wives who was homesick for her Persian birthplace. Babylon lies south of Baghdad in modern Iraq.

Barnsdale Drive   Barnsdale Gardens in Rutland were famously cultivated on television by Geoff Hamilton when he was presenting BBC's 'Gardeners World'. Since his death in 1996 Barnsdale has been open to the public and many plants propagated from the gardens may be bought at the nursery.

Benmore Rise   Near Dunoon in Scotland, Benmore Gardens cover some 140 acres of woodland. There is an avenue of giant redwood trees and a large collection of rhododendrons. The gardens are managed by the Royal Botanic Garden of Edinburgh.

Berrington Grove   Lancelot 'Capability' Brown landscaped the grounds of Berrington Hall near Leominster, Herefordshire before his son-in-law, Henry Holland, designed the house in the late 18th century. The walled garden has an orchard of 50 varieties of pre-1900 apple trees.

Bodnant Court   The 80 acres of garden at Bodnant Hall near Colwyn Bay in Wales are divided into two parts. Close to the house the upper garden is terraced with tree-shaded lawns, while the lower garden, or Dell, contains the Wild Garden. There are plants from all over the world, chosen to suit the Welsh climate and soil.

Brantwood Close   Beside Coniston Water in Cumbria, Brantwood was the home of John Ruskin, the Victorian writer and art critic. In the Professor's Garden, Ruskin experimented with native flowers and fruit and today it has been recreated in the spirit of beauty and productivity he favoured. The Zig-zag Garden is designed round the theme of Dante's Purgatoria and the Fern Garden contains a collection of 300 ferns.

Bretby Chase   The 600 acres of parkland surrounding Bretby Hall in Derbyshire once contained ornamental gardens reputed to have been second only to Versailles. Created by the 2nd Earl of Chesterfield, only the lakes remain. The walled garden now has six new homes built on it and the Hall is undergoing refurbishment to provide apartments and terrace houses.

Cawdor Rise   Cawdor Castle in Scotland, featured in Shakespeare's *Macbeth*, is still the home of the Cawdor family whose ancestors built it in the 14th century. By the stream the wild garden has trails through mature woodland and the restored walled garden contains a holly maze, a paradise garden, knot garden and thistle garden.

Chiswick Close   Chiswick House in London was built by Lord Burlington and is regarded as one of the finest Palladian villas in England. The 18th-century gardens range from majestic cedar trees to the more formal Italianate garden with its temples, statues, obelisks and cascading water.

Cliveden Place   The extensive gardens of Cliveden near Taplow in Berkshire contain a variety of formal and informal gardens, with herbaceous borders, a topiary and water garden. The collection of statues, which includes Roman antiquities collected by 1st Viscount Astor, is one of the most important in the care of the National Trust.

Cranborne Avenue   The 17th-century gardens of Cranborne Manor in Dorset were rediscovered in the 19th century. They were originally designed by Mounten Jennings with plants supplied by John Tradescant. In springtime the crab apple trees in blossom and the display of spring bulbs are particularly beautiful.

Dartington Place   The 14th-century mansion of Dartington Hall near Totnes, Devon is surrounded by 28 acres of landscaped gardens. The Hall was built by John Holland, Earl of Huntingdon, between 1388-99. Half-brother to Richard II, he later became Duke of Exeter.

Docton Mill   Docton Mill and Garden is in Spekes Valley, Hartland, Devon. Set in eight acres of wooded valley with a working mill, the all seasons garden is open to the public from March to the end of October.

Earlshall Place   The gardens of Earlshall Castle in north-east Fife, Scotland, were rescued from ruin and redesigned by Sir Robert Lorimer between 1891-8. There is a rose garden, secret garden, orchard and a croquet lawn plus an elaborate topiary of yew chessmen, shaped from mature trees rescued by Lorimer from an abandoned Edinburgh garden.

Edzell Crescent   Edzell Castle and Garden is in Angus, Scotland. The walled garden created by Sir David Lindsay in 1604 is regarded as one of Scotland's unique sites. The walls of the formal garden are decorated with flower boxes and have niches for nesting birds.

Exbury Lane   Exbury Gardens, Southampton, is owned by Edmund de Rothschild. Two hundred acres of woodland contain the Rothschild collection of rhododendrons, azaleas and camellias. There are also ponds, cascades, a rose garden and rock garden.

Frampton Grove   Frampton Court and Frampton Manor in Gloucestershire are both owned by the Clifford family who were granted the land in 1066 by William the Conqueror. Frampton Court, by Vanbrugh, has a gothic orangery in the garden and the Elizabethan Frampton Manor has a walled garden, a granary and dovecote.

Frogmore Place   The gardens of Frogmore House in the Home Park of Windsor Castle are renowned for their atmosphere of peace and beauty. Queen Victoria wrote: 'All is peace and quiet and you only hear the humming of the bees, the singing of the birds.'

Goldney Court   The mid-18th-century garden of Goldney Hall near Bristol is famed for its lead statue of Hercules, which was erected in 1758. Also in the garden are an ornamental canal, a gothic tower, a rotunda and a grotto.

Hidcote Drive   In the grounds of a thatched house, Hidcote Manor Garden at Chipping Campden, Gloucestershire is divided with walls and hedges into a series of smaller gardens, each with its own character. Considered one of England's best Arts and Crafts gardens, it was designed by American horticulturalist Lawrence Johnston, who bought Hidcote Manor in 1907 and lived there until 1948 when it was acquired by the National Trust.

Heligan Place   The award-winning Lost Gardens of Heligan in Cornwall were uncovered by a violent storm in 1990, which exposed the remains of 19th-century gardens abandoned in 1914 with the outbreak of the First World War. Once the seat of the Tremayne family, a large part of the gardens has been restored and work is still in progress.

Inverewe Place   Owned by the National Trust for Scotland, Inverewe Garden beside the loch at Poolewe, Ross and Cromarty has the tallest Australian gum trees in Britain as well as exotic Chilean trees, Blue Nile lilies and Chinese rhododendrons flourishing in such a northerly climate because Inverewe benefits from the warm current of the North Atlantic Drift.

Killerton Place   Killerton House near Exeter, Devon has a hillside garden with flowering bulbs in spring, colourful herbaceous borders and trees and shrubs. Park and woodland walks surround the house. It is owned by the National Trust.

Leonardslee   In Horsham, Sussex, Leonardslee Gardens are one of the largest woodland gardens in England. A spectacular display of azaleas, rhododendrons, shrubs and trees line seven lakes in a 240-acre valley. The gardens were laid out by Sir Edmund Loder in the early 19th century and are still maintained by the Loder family.

Levens Hall Drive   The Topiary Gardens of Levens Hall at Kendal, Cumbria are world-famous. There are 90 individual pieces of topiary, some reaching almost 300 feet. The designs have remained virtually unchanged since they were laid out in 1694 by Monsieur Beaumont.

Mapperton Close   A Jacobean manor, Mapperton at Beaminster, Dorset is owned by the Earl and Countess of Sandwich. The Italianate garden has an orangery, topiary and formal borders leading down to fish ponds. The house and gardens have featured in 'Emma' and 'Tom Jones' and in the television programme 'Restoration'.

Miserden Crescent   Misarden Park Gardens stand high above the 'Golden Valley' near Stroud, Gloucestershire. There are fine displays of topiary, flowering trees and bulbs in spring, double herbaceous borders in summer and a rose garden with hebes, aliums and lavender recently added.

Nuneham Grove   The Harcourt Arboretum near Nuneham Courtenay, Oxfordshire is owned and run by the Oxford University Botanic Gardens. Occupying part of Nuneham Park Estate, which was owned by the Harcourt family from 1712, the first tree planting began in 1835, the original

Arboretum being designed by William Sawrey Gilpin in the 'picturesque' style. It was sold to the University in 1955. With the help of a grant from Defra's Countryside Stewardship Scheme, access for wheelchair users has been much improved.

Nymans Gate   Owned by the National Trust, Nymans Garden near Haywards Heath in Sussex boasts a profusion of rare and beautiful plants, shrubs and trees from all over the world. There are woodland walks, a hidden sunken garden, pinetum and laurel walk as well as a walled garden.

Powis Lane   Powis Castle and Garden near Welshpool, north Wales, is another National Trust property. Rare and tender plants in the herbaceous borders are sheltered by large, overhanging clipped yew trees. The layout of the garden was influenced by the French and Italian styles and has an orangery and its original lead statues.

Rushfields Close   Rushfields is a garden centre at Ledbury in Herefordshire.

Savill Lane   Savill Garden in Windsor Great Park, Berkshire is owned by The Crown Estate. The 35-acre woodland garden attracts visitors from all over the world to see its all-year-round traditional displays: daffodils in spring, through rhododendron, azaleas and camellias to roses in summer and the trees in their autumn glory.

Sissinghurst Drive   The garden of Sissinghurst Castle at Cranbrook, Kent was created by Vita Sackville-West and her husband, Sir Harold Nicolson. Like outdoor rooms, a series of enclosed alcoves offer a variety of designs and colours throughout the spring and summer. Central to the whole is a red brick prospect tower and walls, the remains of an Elizabethan mansion.

Stapeley Court   Stapeley Water Gardens near Nantwich, Cheshire is both a display garden and the world's largest water garden centre. The Palms Tropical Oasis has tropical and Mediterranean plants flowering beneath the palm trees, giant waterlilies, piranha and other tropical fish, macaws and Toco Toucans among many other plants and creatures. Stapeley is also the home of the National Collection of Nymphae.

Stoneleigh Court   Founded in the reign of Henry II, Stoneleigh Abbey at Kenilworth, Warwickshire later passed to the Duke of Suffolk, then to the Leigh family who owned it for 400 years. It is now owned by a charitable trust. The 690 acres of garden and parkland have been influenced by several landscape architects, including Humphry Repton.

Stourhead Gate   Stourhead at Stourton in Wiltshire is renowned as an outstanding example of the English landscape style of garden. It was laid out between 1741 and 1780 to designs by Henry Hoare II and includes classical temples such as the Pantheon and Temple of Apollo set in the trees around the lake.

Wimborne Crescent   At Hampreston, between Wimborne and Ferndown in Dorset, Knoll is a six-acre award-winning garden which features 6,000 plants from all over the world, as well as the National Collections of phygelius and ceanothus. Two minutes' walk from the centre of Wimborne Minster, Dean's Court is a 13-acre partly wild garden, featuring trees, lawns, and a kitchen garden, all with chemical-free plants. Also at Wimborne Minster, Wimborne Model Town and Gardens is a recreation in miniature of a typical English rural market town in the 1950s. As well as the miniature gardens, there is the Sunflower Garden putting lawn, a children's play area and cream teas in the grounds.

Wroxton Court   Wroxton Abbey Garden near Banbury, Oxfordshire contains the remains of formal gardens created between 1723-32 by Tilleman Bobart and a Rococo scheme by Sanderson Miller created for Lord North in about 1739. There is a serpentine lake, a Doric temple and a dovecote resembling a gothic tower among other attractions.

WOODHILL

Woodhill was the historic name for the area lying between Oakhill and Shenley Woods, with a large field named Wood Common listed in 1693. It is now the site of Woodhill prison.

Wisewood Road   Giving access to the prison, this road name possibly alludes to the 'wise' owls which haunt the woods.

SELECT BIBLIOGRAPHY

AA Book of British Villages, Drive Publication Ltd, 1980

AA Illustrated Guide to Britain, Drive Publications Ltd, 1971

AA Leisure Guide to Devon and Exmoor, AA Publishing, 2002

Chambers Biographical Dictionary, 1986

The How it Works Encyclopaedia of Great Inventors & Discoveries, Marshall Cavendish Books Ltd, 1978

Kerrod, Robin, *Purnell's Concise Encyclopaedia of Science*, Purnell & Sons Ltd, 1974

Markham, Sir Frank, *History of Milton Keynes and District*, White Crescent Press, 1973

Norfolk and the Broads, A Ward Lock Red Guide, Ward Lock Ltd, 1973

Porter, Lindsey, *The Peak District*, 1984

South Cornwall, Red Guide, Ward, Lock & Co. Ltd (15th edition)

South-East Coast, A Ward Lock Red Guide, Ward Lock Ltd, 1974

Useful Websites

English Heritage: www.english-heritage.org.uk

Exmoor National Park Authority: www.exmoor-nationalpark.gov.uk

The Country Lovers' Website: www.Countrylovers.co.uk

The National Trust: www.nationaltrust.org.uk

Illustration acknowledgements:

Buckinghamshire Archives, 56 (top); National Portrait Gallery, London, 55; Milton Keynes Development Corporation, pages 36, 51. Other photographs are by the author.